"Alan Roxburgh is a father figure to many of us in the missional movement and like everything he writes, this is a smart book and a wise one. Defending the importance of structures for mission, he calls us to stop naively pouring our energy into trying to change institutions as an end in itself. Rather, he insists we need to change the narratives that shape the structures that will in turn foster the rich, organic, local missional community we all crave."

Michael Frost, Morling College, Sydney, author of *The Road to Missional*

"Cultural change is more painful than cosmetic change. But if the church in its local, regional and national expressions is going to move into God's future, we must be willing to question our underlying assumptions and provide space to re-imagine. Alan Roxburgh reorients us to seeing God as primary agent and gives us practical help in how to move from a 'manage and control' approach to discerning the work of the Spirit in the local. The question is: Are we willing to live by faith?"

JR Woodward, national director, V3 Church Planting Movement, and author of *Creating a Missional Culture*

"'Forget old structures, let's focus on effective strategies, or let's emerge, or let's be organic. . . . ' Alan Roxburgh names the romanticism and misplaced tactics that trap our anxious imaginations and instead calls for patient theological refection, spiritual discernment and experimental practices. The narratives underneath our structures (in both church and society) are powerful and in flux, and such shifts are about legitimacy, loyalty and how we can participate with God when so much seems tenuous. Roxburgh knows the terrain and is once again a resourceful, engaging, reliable guide."

Mark Lau Branson, Fuller Theological Seminary, coeditor of *Starting Missional Churches: Life with God in the Neighborhood*

"For me, the doctrine of Christ's incarnation is mostly about God entering a particular zip code. Jesus didn't come everywhere; he came somewhere. And that 'where' is within the certain structures and institutions of a given place. Jesus went to the temple. And Jesus turned the tables over in the temple. He came to structures to change structures. Alan Roxburgh has, for years, resurrected the Western church's need to examine the inescapable relationship between place and mission. God entered time and space. A placeless God is the god of the deists, not of Christianity. And here, once again, we are provoked to prod, push and consider this relationship once again. If God entered a zip code, shouldn't we as well?"

A. J. Swoboda, pastor, professor and author of *A Glorious Dark*

"In this clarion call, Alan Roxburgh makes a robust case that most efforts to 'fix our church' are doomed to fail. Instead, *Structured for Mission* invites leaders on a journey to experience how God's renewal of neighborhoods and churches shouldn't ever be separated."

Tim Soerens, cofounding director of the Parish Collective and coauthor of *The New Parish*

"A groundbreaking book on church structure that creatively explores the deeper realities of the structures we inhabit by unpacking the importance of legitimizing narratives. Roxburgh insightfully deconstructs the modern, corporate denomination that was largely about structures of command and control. But he proposes a way forward by inviting church leaders to cultivate a biblical imagination and to utilize Spirit-led discernment to engage in experiments in order to discover new practices of structure that focus on the local, distributive systems and networking. A must-read for church leaders across the spectrum of denominations—local, regional and national."

Craig Van Gelder, emeritus professor of congregational mission, Luther Seminary

"All future iterations of church structure will pass through this must-read book by Alan Roxburgh. With intellectual breadth, wisdom and clarity Roxburgh explores deep formative questions exposing how our church institutions and structures organize our lives and can be renewed, even transformed. All structures are embedded with narratives and traditions. The future of church structures requires both theological imagination and discernment with the Spirit to realign those narratives and traditions with God's dream for creation thus rendering more plausible material expression in everyday life. I commend *Structured for Mission* to you."

Dwight J. Friesen, associate professor of practical theology at The Seattle School of Theology & Psychology, coauthor of *The New Parish* and *Routes and Radishes*, and author of *Thy Kingdom Connected*

"The churches of North America, especially those of Eurotribal descent, face unprecedented challenges in our day. As Roxburgh helps us to see, these challenges are not the sort that will be meaningfully addressed by more/bigger/better tactics and strategies, but rather through the development of fresh imagination and new narratives that take shape at the local level. This is a book that can help all of us who lead denominations, networks and Christian institutions navigate this difficult-but-necessary journey in God's mission."

JR Rozko, codirector, Missio Alliance

Alan J. Roxburgh

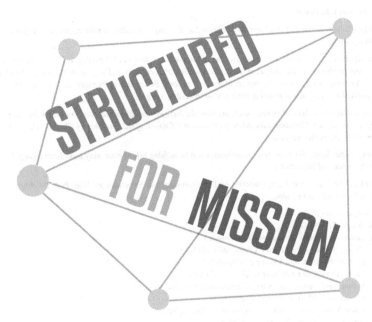

RENEWING THE CULTURE OF THE CHURCH

IVP Books

An imprint of InterVarsity Press
Downers Grove, Illinois

InterVarsity Press
P.O. Box 1400, Downers Grove, IL 60515-1426
ivpress.com
email@ivpress.com

InterVarsity Press® is the book-publishing division of InterVarsity Christian Fellowship/USA®, a movement of
students and faculty active on campus at hundreds of universities, colleges and schools of nursing in the United
States of America, and a member movement of the International Fellowship of Evangelical Students. For
information about local and regional activities, visit intervarsity.org.

Scripture quotations, unless otherwise noted, are from the New Revised Standard Version of the Bible, copyright
1989 by the Division of Christian Education of the National Council of the Churches of Christ in the USA. Used
by permission. All rights reserved.

While any stories in this book are true, some names and identifying information may have been changed to
protect the privacy of individuals.

Figure 11.1, The Great River Park, rendering by Ben Thompson and Associates for Saint Paul Riverfront
Corporation. Used by permission.

Cover design: Cindy Kiple
Interior design: Beth McGill
Images: Senior Asian man: © quavondo/iStockphoto
        Young African girl: © Peeter Viisimaa/iStockphoto
        Man on the street: © halbergman/iStockphoto
        Young woman: © DRB Images, LLC/iStockphoto
        Indian rural women: © Anantha Vardhan/iStockphoto
        African man: © AfricaImages/iStockphoto
        Young Indian man: © Vikram Raghuvanshi/iStockphoto
        Distraught women: © azndc/iStockphoto

ISBN 978-0-8308-4424-1 (print)
ISBN 978-0-8308-9858-9 (digital)

Printed in the United States of America ♾

g **green** As a member of the Green Press Initiative, InterVarsity Press is committed to protecting
press the environment and to the responsible use of natural resources. To learn more, visit
INITIATIVE greenpressinitiative.org.

Library of Congress Cataloging-in-Publication Data
Roxburgh, Alan J.
  Structured for mission : renewing the culture of the church / Alan J. Roxburgh.
      pages cm
  Includes bibliographical references and index.
  ISBN 978-0-8308-4424-1 (pbk. : alk. paper)
  1. Church renewal. I. Title.
  BV600.3.R69 2015
  262.001'7--dc23
                                                                              2015013543

P   21   20   19   18   17   16   15   14   13   12   11   10   9   8   7   6   5   4   3   2   1
Y   33   32   31   30   29   28   27   26   25   24   23   22   21   20   19   18   17   16   15

This book is dedicated to my friend and colleague

Craig Van Gelder.

Craig has been a mentor in my formation and intellectual development. I have learned so much from him in terms of systems, change and good process design. Without his insights and our long conversations, this book would not have formed in my imagination. Craig has also been a good friend with whom I have been able to confide. He has always been available. His advice has been not just wise but also spoken with a deep care for me. This kind of friendship is rare. I'm deeply grateful for him and our journey together over more than a quarter century.

Contents

Contents

PART ONE

THE LOSS OF PLACE

The Place of Structures in the Midst of Massive Change

INTRODUCTION: THREE STRUCTURES, THREE STORIES

Structures are a common part of our everyday lives. You are likely reading this book sitting at home, in an office or at a coffee shop. Each is a building structured to address a certain set of habits and practices that shape our lives. These buildings house our different roles. We usually take them for granted. They've always been there for us. Structures are, however, rich containers and shapers of meaning for us. Take, for example, figures 1.1, 1.2 and 1.3. The cathedral (fig. 1.1), high-rise (fig. 1.2) and suburb (fig. 1.3) each express a different story about how communities of people in different times structured their lives. The cathedral takes us back to the Middle Ages, the high-rise represents the heyday of modernism in urban architecture, and the suburb reflects the dominant way in which most of us live today.

Each of these three structures tells its own story about what the people in each of these periods believed was important for their thriving together. The cathedral lay at the center of a society. Its structure told the story of the Christian narrative and the human journey. In its shadow people were formed inside a story about how life was best lived. The high-rise came to dominate urban landscapes at the beginning of the twentieth century. It represented a totally different story about how we thrive as communities. It was the rationalized, planned living space designed for efficiency through the separation of work, commerce and private lives. Finally, the suburb embodies yet another vastly different story about how we thrive. Its structuring is about the individual as the center of all meaning; it connotes independence, self-development and autonomy.

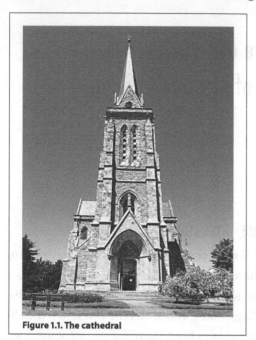

Figure 1.1. The cathedral

Three structures. Each created inside very different stories about how human beings thrive. Structures are the embodiment of meaning. They are the ways we take wood, stone, glass, steel, concrete, plastic or an organizational chart and form them to express our deepest convictions about what is important in life and how we believe life is made to work. There is nothing neutral or taken for granted about structures.

We are in a time when many long-established forms of church life are unraveling. Figure 1.4, for example, is of a church in a West Coast neighborhood where more people describe their religious affiliation as "none" than attend churches. Back in the middle of the twentieth century when someone passed this structure, he or she would have been completely at home identifying what it meant and its place in his or her life. Today that happens

Figure 1.2. The high-rise

far less! Now it symbolizes a quaint structure people pass on their way to somewhere else; it's mostly a structure from the past few remember.

The temptation is to think that the primary cause for this unraveling is existing structures. With this assumption in place it seems reasonable to believe that by creating new structures or restructuring existing forms the problem will be solved. This is why, over the past half-century, we have seen multiple proposals for remaking the church. But what if there is something else going on? Perhaps we need to understand why and how we create and become committed to certain structures in order to discern

Figure 1.3. The suburb

how to address the unraveling? If we take the time to ask about the reasons for the structures we have created, as well as the alternative ones we propose to take the place of existing structures, perhaps we can discern the ways the Spirit is gestating new life in the midst of current institutions and structures.

Our changing situation: Unraveling. North American society is in the midst of massive change. Change is always with us and, as such, is nothing new. The character of the change we face is its speed, unpredictability and multiplicity—it's not just one or two elements that are changing, but it seems like practically everything is up for grabs. There is an attendant recognition that many of the churches are struggling to get handles on the implications of these changes for their own identity, mission and ministry. The situation is particularly challenging for those Protestant churches that are the inheritors of the European reformations of the sixteenth century and European migrations that followed. These Eurotribal churches, until recently the dominant forms of church in North America, still represent a major form of Christian life. However, a way of being, leading and organizing the church is unraveling. The unraveling metaphor proposes that existing ways of being church are less and less able to provide meaningful ways of shaping people's religious life.

The drive to address this situation is understandable. A pressing question is how to respond effectively to this situation. What are the most helpful approaches? How do the Eurotribal churches understand

Figure 1.4. West Vancouver United Church

and engage their massive unraveling? In seeking to get bearings and find effective ways of responding, it may not be helpful to assume that the primary need is to change institutions, reframe structures or even renew long-established practices. This book explains why and proposes a different way of addressing the unraveling. To get some perspective on the challenges facing the churches, it is helpful to summarize some of the sources of the massive changes affecting our society at so many levels. What follows is not an exhaustive characterization but a selection of several areas undergoing massive transformation (there are many others, and therein is the crisis we face—the multilevel and multidimensional nature of the change) as illustrative of the challenges facing the churches and undermining so much of their current forms and practices.

Economics. Few of us would doubt that over the past several years economic foundations have been badly shaken. The result, for many, is a massive uncertainty and anxiety about their own and children's economic future. The taken-for-granted dream that anyone who works and tries hard enough in this society can "make it" has evaporated. Even before the economic implosion of 2008 there was a restive sense that the rules of how we earn a living and secure our future were rapidly changing. Words like *globalization* and *postindustrial* had already presaged a very different and scary period for many in terms of their economic future. The ever-widening earning gap between the rich and the rest said that something was deeply out of sync with the way the economic world had worked in the recent past. The French economist Thomas Piketty's hefty new book *Capital in the Twenty-First Century* undoes the myth of the trickle-down theory that enervated neo-conservative economic theory, and shows that we have entered a new era wherein wage earners will continually fall behind as the economic assumptions that shaped most of the twentieth century no longer function.

In his book *The End of Growth*, Jeff Rubin describes a series of powerful global forces now rearranging our assumptions about growth and therefore work. He points out that while the 2008 global recession was tough, it was more like a concussion than the real issue. These are not comforting words for most of us as we watch what was once called the middle class get ever smaller. The shape of our economic lives, and that of our children and grandchildren, is very much up for grabs. Rubin argues something is happening that's fundamentally changing the economic realities we have lived in. He sees national governments in the West continuing to cling to the notion that we are recovering from a blip and that good times are just about ready to return. But there is a growing sense among us that something deep and fundamental has shifted. He views the basic reality we're facing in terms of the end of growth. This is a massive disruption, since growth has been the economic assumption we have operated from. Oil is the engine driving the economies of the West. Even as the price of oil plummeted in late 2014 and will likely stay this way for a year or two, the underlying reality that oil is a limited com-

modity that is ever more expensive to extract will not change in the mid-
to long term. These new sources of oil (deep well drilling, shale extraction, tar sands) are only viable at current cost levels. They are viable
because of the current high cost of oil production and therefore are themselves contributors to the end of growth.

This scenario of the end of growth may not be the complete picture,
but at this point in time it is becoming a viable explanation for the slow,
imperceptible "recovery" characterizing the economies of the West. The
result is the slowing of real job growth along with stagnation in real
wages (adjusted to inflation). The reality for many coming out of college
is the difficulty of finding work. So many entry-level jobs pay so little
that they can't begin to address educational debt and drive young adults
back into their parents' homes.

What do these economic shifts mean for being the church? This is not
meant to be an economic treatise but an illustration of the massive
changes contributing to the unraveling of the churches as we have known
them. For multiple generations Protestant churches were successful because their members had steady, secure jobs with things like pension
plans, vacations and sick days. Most of these churches were populated
by the now-shrinking middle classes, most of whom had 9-to-4 jobs and
weekends off. These economic realities meant that the churches were
shaped by a huge reservoir of volunteerism that runs programs, as well
as people with sufficient and predictable incomes to give. This world has
disappeared. Emerging generations no longer have the weekends or the
paid vacations or the health plans. Most young adults will have had three
to five jobs by the time they reach their late thirties.[1] Most of those jobs
will require them to learn new skills and change their patterns of life. The
world these adults now live in is no longer neatly divided between work,
home life and pleasure. The competition for jobs linked with the ubiqui-
tousness of technology means work is now a 24/7 fact of life with little
time left over for anything else except one's small coterie of friends. In
the new economy there is little time left over for church and all the ways
it has been programmed. Volunteerism is a luxury for the few, hardly
something most can afford to give. These are massive changes across
society that challenge some of the most basic ways in which the Prot-

estant churches have operated over the past fifty or more years.

Family. When *All in the Family* and Archie Bunker represented the modern family in the 1970s, it pushed the edges of the "traditional" family, but all the parameters of that imagination were still firmly in place. When Cameron and Mitchell appear on the current *Modern Family* one knows that any pretense to some idea of a traditional family has gone. We are in new territory. Families just aren't what they used to be. More and more young adults remain at home longer and longer because of the economic transformations noted earlier. But even more significant, there are increasing numbers of people who are living alone. One of the largest emerging demographics are people living on their own. Today, "family" has an amorphous, shifting identity in which the classic (nineteenth- and twentieth-century European and North American ideal of the nuclear family—a father, mother and 2.5 children) understanding is more like an endangered species than the norm. Fewer adults make marriage vows, greater numbers choose to live as one-parent families, blended families are normal, and children learn to live in different homes shared between parents in agreed upon legal arrangements where they have multiple sets of brothers and sisters.

The terminology of *marriage* and *family* is difficult to navigate. What does a church mean when it advertises a "Family Camp" or hires a new staff person to run a "Family Ministry" program? Church used to be one of those primary places where people met their future partners; now a significant percentage meet online through dating services, Christian or otherwise. Contemporary marriage is based more and more on voluntary commitment (rather than covenant) with fewer and fewer children. An unintended consequence is that these small units with tenuous connections to extended families and others forms of support are under huge stress from the massive economic and social changes overrunning their capacities to cope.

For a hundred or more years Protestant congregations have been built around what has come to be known as the *nuclear* family. The ethos, language, programs and often unexpressed assumptions of congregations are still built around this understanding of family. It is incredibly difficult for leaders to know how to navigate these treacherous waters when people are divided about what is right and what is wrong in terms of being family. Not so long ago there were straightforward formulas for running generationally segmented, family-based programs. This was the basis of a successful ministry. Today, fewer and fewer congregations can make this work when the families in their neighborhoods bear little resemblance to this imagination.

Again, the description of *family* is intended to be illustrative of yet another element in the massive changes moving across society. As with the economic challenge, so it is with the family challenge. The middle-class economic model of the last half of the twentieth century, upon which a whole way of being the church was designed, has all but gone. In a parallel manner, the whole edifice of being family which these churches were built around is rapidly coming apart. These Eurotribal churches are being confronted not simply with a single tough, intractable challenge, they're confronting multiple intractable challenges all at once that question some of the most basic convictions about how a society ought to function. One further illustration will be sufficient to show how this is now the normative situation for the Eurotribal churches.

Diversity. At the beginning of the new millennium Diana Eck published a book, *A New Religious America*, in which she proposed that while American Protestants where engaged in their culture wars, a sea change had been underway in the diversity of religious life. She wrote,

> There are more Muslim Americans than Episcopalians, more Muslims than members of the Presbyterian Church USA. . . . We are astonished to learn that Los Angeles is the most complex Buddhist city in the world. . . .
>
> [M]ake no mistake: in the last thirty years, as Christianity has become more publicly vocal, something else of enormous importance has happened. The United States has become the most religiously diverse nation on earth.[2]

Several years ago Joel Kotkin wrote a book about an America that has grown from 300 million at the end of the first decade of the twenty-first century to 400 million by the midpoint of the century. The origins of the peoples making up that next 100 million will not be like the majority Eurotribal people who have comprised America to this point. They will be people from Asia, the Middle East and a host of other non-European locations. America will be once more in a process of reinventing itself for this radically new geography of diversity. Some kind of hybridization of American culture will emerge that will likely look, feel and act very differently from the current tribal enclaves that have tended to shape urban growth over the past sixty or more years. Even at this point in North American history, the younger generations are increasingly multiracial in relationships. They are less and less aware of or shaped by differences of race, ethnicity, sexuality or religious preference. Already there is a pronounced shift to multirace and even multifaith marriages, a sharp turn from a more recent time when race and religion were deciding factors in the choice of a partner.

Up until the present moment Protestant congregations across North America have been predominantly monocultural groups whose programs, worship forms and ethos have been designed around the dominance of Eurotribal traditions. All of this is being challenged by the changes cataloged by Eck and Kotkin. This is not an accusation directed toward these churches, but recognition of yet one more massive, disruptive sociocultural transformation that has to be faced. Forms of leadership, structures and institutions that have supported these churches so well for so long are now faced with yet another shaking of their foundations. Denominational structures that have shaped Protestant churches along with multiple other forms of Eurotribal church life have continually illustrated a certain kind of religious diversity among themselves. But this has largely been a diversity based on Eurotribal differences and the capacity of the various Eurotribal churches to continually find creative ways of adapting to changing contexts. The diversity described in this section is of a fundamentally different kind. It takes these churches into a new, off-the-map world. A new immigrant Christianity is emerging that will bring with it practices, values and theologies that won't fit neatly into the notions of Christian life familiarly shaped by the European reformations in terms of their polities, theologies and forms of communal life. The Protestant churches find themselves needing to travel in yet another altered religious landscape. It represents a great opportunity. These churches have a long tradition of being remarkably adaptable. But it means navigating yet another set of changes.

In summary, existing ways of being church are less and less able to provide meaningful ways of shaping people's religious life in these tumultuous shifts. While the drive to address this situation is understandable, the pressing questions are: How do we respond effectively? How do we understand and engage this context where our given maps don't seem to match the territory we now travel in? In the context of such massive challenges it becomes evident that the structures and institutions that once served us so well are no longer producing the results we have come to expect, or they seem to be a primary block to any real change. The assumption I make, therefore, is that the structures and institutions are themselves the problem and in need of either being changed or discarded. This is why we have witnessed a long period of attempts to restructure our organizational systems, renew established practices or introduce new structures to address changing situations. But are structures and institutions actually the problem? So many of the attempts to renew, restructure and reorganize congregations and denominational systems over the past twenty or more years doesn't seem to have changed the situation of these churches. Is there more going on that needs to be understood before assuming structural and organizational change will address the challenges of disruptive change? To answer that question we need to ask what structures are for.

WHAT ARE STRUCTURES FOR?

Each morning when I am home, a certain set of habits shapes my life. I didn't sit down and plan them out, but they're now built into the rhythms of my life. Around 5:30 a.m. an alarm goes off in my head. I'm ready to get up; sleeping in makes no sense. I go to the kitchen, make my first cup of coffee and head to the office to do a couple of hours of writing or reading. In this sense, my life is ritualized; it's structured by a set of habits or practices. Those early morning hours are highly structured. We all have examples of how patterns and habits shape the rhythms of our lives. For some, Sunday morning offers a reassuring set of events in terms of going to church and entering worship. For good and ill, our lives are shaped by structures that have either been passed down to us through family and education, or we have entered for ourselves. There is no life without structure. In the images of cathedral, apartment building and suburban home introduced earlier, each represents a structured way of life. The suburban home, for example, is designed to provide us with a certain way of living that is quite different from either of the other two structures.

Structures organize or institutionalize our lives. Neither structures, organizations nor institutions are inherently bad. Rather, they're the basic forms through which we live the kinds of lives we believe are important, or into which we were born and hence take for granted as the norm. The recent TV series *Downton Abbey* revolves around a structure that shaped a whole way of life. Its more euphemistic description was "upstairs-downstairs." The image describes how differing social classes lived together in a highly structured environment. The abbey had been built to ensure that the servants and hired help lived on the bottom levels of the building, from which they served the needs of the gentry. These beliefs about the differentiation of class and the roles people were born into was put into the structured, organized forms of the building—the abbey itself was built to institutionalize these cultural values. Behind structures lie these deeper cultural values.

Recently, I developed a new and surprising pain in my lower back after a run. After visiting the doctor I scheduled a one-on-one with a yoga instructor. She sat me in a chair, and after a few exercises placed a small model of the human skeleton between us. She pointed to the bones of the lower spine with their attendant hip joints. Her point was to show me how this combination of bones was intended to work together (structured for optimal health) and how I was working against that structuring of my body, hence the pain. We are formed in biological and social systems structured to give us particular characteristics as groups and persons. We can communicate with one another because our language is structured. The sentences I am writing follow a structured set of patterns that ensure all who read this can understand its content. We *institutionalize* these ways of writing so we can communicate with one another. We take all this for granted. All the varieties of ways we structure our lives (family, buildings, transportation, educational, political, religious and social forms) say something about how we understand the meaning and purpose of our lives. The three structures illustrated at the beginning of this book demonstrate this. We tend to take the structures we live in for granted. In so doing, we don't see their formative power, how they shape the practice of our lives. The fact is, all of life is structured life.

I'm sitting at the kitchen counter with my four-year-old grandson, Adam. He places on the counter a box filled with an assortment of *Star Wars* figures from the original movies of the late 1970s right up to the more recent ones. The figures are in less than pristine condition. Dismembered body parts lie scattered around the box. Not all figures resemble the way they originally came in their boxes. Adam, however, knows how to organize them for his granddad. Returning them to some order is simple for Adam. He pulls a figure out and attaches several pieces (helmets and a colored light saber), giving it a name. "This is a bad guy!" he declares. "Umm!" is my bemused response. Pointing into the box, I ask, "Where is a good guy, then?" With some disdain for my lack of awareness he picks up another figure, takes up another light saber and says to me, "See, Granddad, this is a good guy!" I follow with the obvious question, "But, Adam, how do you know which is a good guy and which is a bad guy?" From the tone of his response, it's obvious I am a lesser being in the realm of *Star Wars*. He answers me with the obvious, "Because!" "Because why?" I respond, and am greeted with, "Granddad, don't you know—these are bad guys and these are good guys" (pointing to specific figures as he spoke). Adam was telling me (not quite in a four-year-old's terms, but it's what he was saying), "Granddad, I live inside a story, a narrative structure that has given me all the information and knowledge I need to know about which are the good guys and which the bad ones. My dad has sat and read to me the *Star Wars* stories, so it's obvious which is which. Why don't you recognize the obvious?" Adam's assembling of body parts and his conversation with me reflect his living in a structured narrative within which he orders reality. Structures are essential to life.

In a similar way, organizations are structured narratives that shape how we see our world and relate to others. They are not incidental, like clothes we put on and then cast off for another set, but critical elements shaping our everyday life. They're more than colored LEGO® pieces that can be changed on a whim. There is far more going on with structures than we often imagine.

In discussions about the crisis of the churches, it is interesting to note how the language of "structure" is used in relationship to other words. The language used for existing structures, for example, is often "institution." But the word *institution* often is used in a negative sense as in "institutional church." The term *institutional church* then signals something negative, or less than adequate, about these structures. The combination *institutional structures* functions as a shorthand intimating that existing church structures are the problem and the solution involves replacing them with more relevant structures. Such proposals assume that this sloughing off of existing structures and their replacement with new ones is quite straightforward, with few long-term consequences. Social systems don't operate this way.

Psychoanalyst and philosopher Cornelius Castoriadis (1922–1997) argues that to be human is by definition to be set inside institutions that operate as structured forms of social life. For him, institutions cannot be reduced to problematic accretions that stand in our way, but are essential for human thriving. A society is knit together—becomes a fabric of social interactions—through its institutions. In this way institutions are the structured embodiment of the core narratives of a group of people. Every person is the product of institutions formed within intricately structured webs of institutionalized relationships interacting with one another to produce a complex tapestry of connections. Over long periods of time, societies cohere within perduring institutional structures that become the implicit forms of everyday life (e.g., the medieval cathedral or guild or weekly market; the modern places of association in clubs, sports arenas or shopping malls). Such structures can display amazing cohesion (the church in Europe, for example, exists right up to the present even though its functions have changed dramatically) over long periods of time, through an incredible array of complex rules, differentiation of roles, customs, habits and practices. The family, in its many forms, is an institutional structure. When such structuring of common life shapes a society over a long period of time, these structures come to be taken for granted; they are the accepted norms.

STRUCTURE AND CHANGE

The relationship between structures and change is complex. Sometimes, structures robustly thrive through massive amounts of traumatic change over a long period of time, and then, in what seems like a moment, collapse for seemingly innocuous reasons. The fall of Rome or collapse of the communist Eastern Block each illustrate this reality. Why do certain moments of change bring down long-established structures, while other periods of chaotic change leave existing structures in place? The reasons are not simple, nor are they easy to explain. The cathedral is now a tourist destination, not that central structure that once provided a coherent narrative shaping people's lives. The modern skyscraper is no longer viewed as the best structure for housing people. The suburb is under intense pressure as more of us question its promise of a healthy way of life in the midst of human isolation and environmental degradation. The guild system that once dominated European social structure collapsed before the emergence of a nascent capitalism in the seventeenth century. Feudalism could not withstand early industrialization or expanding empires with their need for trade.

I recently took a train from Birmingham to London. As the train moved through city, town and countryside, I saw a continual assortment of church spires rising upward into the sky. Not long ago these structures signaled a thriving religious landscape. Today, most of these spires symbolize empty buildings and a long withdrawal of religious vitality. Long-established patterns of social life structurally embedded in cherished institutions come apart. Scouting (founded by Robert Baden-Powell around the time of the Boer War as an initiation into manhood as warrior) was once a major organizational structure for the formation of young men. It quickly lost relevance and membership in the last third of the twentieth century. The church was a dominant institutional structure of the West through to the first half of the twentieth century, when that dominance began to evaporate. It is now increasingly irrelevant to large percentages of people across Europe and North America.

There are no simple explanations for why these shifts occur. What is clear, however, is that the structures that form us in societies are more than extraneous overlays people can pick up and put off with ease. This myth can prevent us from asking the deeper questions of why structures change and what is involved in that change. I write this en route from Vancouver to Chicago. After it seemed everyone was aboard and we were ready to depart, a large family of seven children and two parents raced on board. They were Amish traveling to a wedding in Pennsylvania. As one of the young girls sat beside me and talked while I was writing, it struck me that here was a family formed inside a perduring social structure despite all the beguiling change that surrounds them.

This complexity is important to keep in mind when explaining the massive unraveling through which the churches of the West are moving. Explanations that assume structures are little more than an external dressing that can be cast off on a whim to be replaced with new clothes inhibit our capacity to understand what is at stake or discern how social systems change. This capacity to understand what is happening will be critical to discerning a way forward for these churches. In the massive shifts now transforming our society and unraveling so much of the church's life, structures and institutions play a significant role, but what is that role and how do we address the changes confronting the churches?

The late twentieth and early twenty-first centuries have been times of incredible disruption. Long-established institutional structures are coming apart. People have less and less faith in the ability of political, social, economic and religious structures to solve the problems we are facing, especially in terms of economic and ecological thriving. While still too close to these disruptions to have any clear perspective, several observations can be made about structure and change in terms of current church life.

First, deep divisions exist within and across denominational systems over how to address their unraveling. Tensions exist between those seeking the preservation or renewal of established structures and those pronouncing their replacement. In the Church of England, for example, Fresh Expressions suggests the church grows in places where people experiment with new structures, while others counterpropose the power of traditional structures (see *For the Parish*).[3] A similar tension is present in the Roman Catholic Church. Reformers call on a conservative hierarchy to dismantle such institutional structures as celibacy and male-only clergy, while Rome remains firmly committed to them. In North America, denominations such as the Presbyterian Church USA face major internal conflicts around order, structure and the call for new forms of organizational life. Methodists seek to address the unraveling by instituting fresh ways of making existing structures work more efficiently by creating dashboards for church growth.

Second, it is enormously difficult to propose alternative structures in periods of major change. Real caution needs to be placed around proposals for restructuring in the midst of sociocultural disruption. This is not to say action isn't necessary. Congregations and denominations need to embrace huge amounts of change. But what if the kind of change that needs to be addressed isn't primarily organizational or structural? What if there are much more powerful, underlying issues at stake? Perhaps there are good reasons for a sober cautiousness toward all those demanding such change? We are living right in the midst of these disruptions. We are, therefore, too much a part of them to see the shape of things to come.

The ending of a bipolar East-West world, symbolized by the fall of the Berlin Wall, illustrates the difficulty. In the late 1970s and early 1980s, we would have been hard pressed to find anyone forecasting the end of this world. Right up to the fall of the Berlin Wall, East German authorities instructing their soldiers to allow citizens through the Brandenburg Gate without the requisite passes had no sense of what would follow. It was an unimagined moment when thousands of Germans from both sides of the divide began pulling down the hated wall. Up to that moment, such actions were inconceivable; they would have been met with volleys of bullets and many deaths. Suddenly a way of life structurally embedded in people's imagination and actions (the Wall) changed. Everyone knew they had entered a different space where the norms, structures and institutions that had shaped them for half a century could not contain what was emerging. As the late president of the Czech Republic, Václav Havel, stated in the 1990s, no one living in the midst of the communist East in the 1970s and 1980s could have imagined such events. Seeing the end of a way of life doesn't privilege us with the capacity to name what will take its place.

From the perspective of 2014, it is clear that any certainty about our capacities to name and create the new structures in this new space is illusory. At multiple levels (social, economic, political and religious) we remain far, far away from any sense of knowing what the structures will be that replace those that disappeared with the fall of the Berlin Wall, with its euphoric conviction of a New World Order and the beginning of a new, blessed future. Does anyone believe any longer that a New World Order has emerged congruent with all the predictions that emerged in the 1990s? It's feeling a lot more like the reemergence of the old Cold War world! Not that long ago the European Union and the Euro were being touted as the third way between American and Chinese economic dominance. No one is making that claim today. The new structures, acclaimed with such expectation for a New World Order and its peace dividend, have given rise to ever higher levels of social, economic and political instability, resulting in more fear and anxiety. New international structures have emerged. Multilateral arrangements, such as the GATT, the G8, the G20 and even the Euro, each broadly acclaimed as the structure of the new era, are failing to bring any kind of stable, secure world order in which people can thrive. The Arab Spring no longer feels like spring. Who can see the shape of things to come?

The initiation of a new wave of globalization in the late 1970s following the breakdown of the established Bretton-Woods agreements on trade (1944) illustrates how rapid social transformation changes established structures and institutions. Practically overnight the narrative convictions shaping economic beliefs were turned on their head. A much vaunted new economic order announced in the 1990s resulted in the financial meltdowns of 2008 and the dawning awareness that, economically, we are in *terra incognita*, not some recovery back to an established norm. The conventional wisdom that framed Bretton-Woods said national economies and their social systems needed to be protected from an international free market in trade and financial transactions. In the first decades of the new millennium, this was cast away with the emergence of a renewed belief in the primacy of the free market and the inviolable force of the invisible hand. This reminted capitalism resulted in nation-states removing practically all their internal controls on the flow of investment monies in and out of their countries, resulting in the rapid restructuring of trade and financial institutions. We may not be sure of the outcomes, but we can be certain that those prognosticators and engineers of this brave new world did not see the shape of things to come. Underlying narratives about how a society thrives can provide structural and institutional stability for a long period and then be suddenly overturned. The disruptions confronting the post-2008 implosion of financial and trade structures is testimony to how nearly impossible it is to write in new organizational and structural systems.

Third, in disruptive change established structures and institutions can quickly lose their capacity to hold people's loyalty. The unraveling of political orders across the Middle East illustrates this. In this level of change a sudden and dramatic shift in the legitimacy of long-standing institutions occurs. *That* this needs to be addressed is clear. *How* it is to be addressed is far less clear. Claiming that changing institutional structures addresses this implosion of legitimacy is patently not the case. The shape of the Middle East has become less clear and more tenuous than ever. The so-called Arab Spring continues to unfold without a sense of what is emerging and how these developments will affect the stability of the world order. Who, at the beginning of 2011, could have imagined the Muslim Brotherhood being the democratically elected government of Egypt? Rather than the visionary pictures of a new world, what quickly happened was the reassertion of the older plutocracy that the so-called Spring had sought to replace. After the Sochi Olympics, conflict between Ukraine and Russia, followed by the seizing of Crimea, pushed the powers back toward the older Cold War era, not a new world. Narratives structured into institutions suddenly cease being tenable for large numbers of a population. As long-established institutional structures come apart (Mubarak's Egypt, Gaddafi's Libya, Assad's Syria, eastern Ukraine), there is little correlation between the ending of some forms and the capacity to know what will take their place. The change cannot be managed primarily through a restructuring or reorganizing. Prophets don't do well in these liminal spaces with proposals around structure and change. That's because the issues lie elsewhere.

Across the churches of the West there are voices, claiming to see what is happening, that propose the elimination of existing structures in favor of their proposed future. Buyer beware! I do not say this as someone wanting to retreat back into a nostalgic embrace of existing structures. In times of high anxiety and confusion, the beguiling voices of the *new* can misguide in unpredictable ways. Structures can't be discarded by declaring their time is over. Nothing in our experience of the past several generations supports this simplistic notion. If changing structures and reinventing institutions was the road to the Promised Land, all churches and denominations would have arrived a long time ago. Other dynamics are at play.

Chapter two will look at some of the other dynamics affecting our existing structures and institutions in order to understand more about how we go about creating the kind of change in congregations and denominations that does engage our new context.

Structures Embody
Our Deeply Held Stories

INTRODUCTION

The delegated members of congregations from a midlevel judicatory were gathered for their annual meeting. They heard, again, the muted statistical report about membership and financial decline from a national officer located in the head office somewhere in the Midwest. Most in attendance were white-haired. Not much was said in the meeting about the actual report; a few perfunctory questions were asked, but the report was received with the appropriate motion and vote, then people moved on to other business. In the coffee klatches after the meeting, however, the questions being asked by these long-time members of this denomination were new: "Why do we have these national offices? What's their point? They take our money and give us nothing in return. Do we really need them anymore?" That such questions are now pervasive across Protestant churches is a massive shift in perspective; it signals a sea change from what these once-loyal church members have believed. Not long ago these denominations, with their professional staffs in national offices, were viewed as essential elements of church life. National structures provided brand name identity, leadership and resources for their congregations.

Over the past thirty years it has become ever more clear that such brand name denominational programs and structures no longer provide identity and purpose to their congregations in the ways they once did. The question is *why*? Chapter one argued that simply stating this fact in order to propose new structures is too simple a response; it fails to get at the question, Why have we spent so much energy and resources in processes of restructuring, reorganizing and renewing, but see little actually change? A key to addressing this question is in understanding what gives structures their ability to provide meaning and direction to a group. This brings us to a term I will use throughout this book: *legitimating narratives*.

What are legitimating narratives? Organizational structures and the institutions they create are expressions of our underlying convictions about what makes life work and what we believe to be important. These underlying convictions and beliefs are a part of what is meant by legitimating narratives. This chapter explains how the organizational structures of our denominational systems and congregations embody and communicate deeply held stories or narratives about what is important and what we believe about being effective and successful. A legitimating narrative is an overarching story that provides a group (a small unit or a whole society) with a way to express its underlying values, beliefs and commitments about who they are and how life is to be lived. It's a story that tells a group who they are, what is acceptable and what is a proper way to live. A few examples will help make this clear. The medieval cathedral, for example, embodied (a built, constructed expression of a culture's deepest convictions about the meaning and purpose of life) a legitimating narrative that shaped European societies through a good part of the Middle Ages. This narrative was, obviously, the Christian story. In that period the great spire(s) of the cathedral continually reminded the citizens living in its environs that all of life was theocentric: God was at the center of and the explanation for all of life. As the spire lifted one's eyes from the ground toward the heavens, one was remind that humans live inside a great chain of being that moved from the earth toward the heavens, where God reigned. This narrative was further expressed inside the cathedral through the structuring of its architecture. The great vaulted arches lifted the eyes toward its massive dome, upon which would be painted the story of Christ's ascension into heaven, where God the Father was painted seated on a throne.

Art and architecture blended to express the central story of life on this earth and our journey toward heaven with Christ. Around the cathedral walls were an array of stained-glass windows, each depicting a story from the Gospels or Epistles about some action of Jesus or the apostles. These were not simply images of adoration but a means of teaching people how to live inside this larger story. A cathedral represented and concretized this legitimating narrative. One final image will round out this picture. Inside many cathedrals, above the immense entrance doors, were painted frescos that worshipers would only see as they were leaving. These frescos depicted human beings falling into hell, with devils and other creatures holding them in bondage and terror. This reminder completed the circle of the narrative by telling people what lay before them in the world if they neglected to follow the story given to them in and by the building itself. The constructed space of the cathedral, its bricks and mortar, frescos, art and windows cohered to provided authority and legitimacy to this version of the Christian story in medieval Europe.

Structures and organizations function in ways that embody and authorize the core narratives of a group or society. Democracy, for example, is a relatively new phenomenon in terms of a primary story driving Western societies. In the seventeenth century John Locke helped to frame the political legitimacy of the democratic process. He argued that it was the consensus of the governed that conferred political legitimacy on those governing. This was a massive transformation from the earlier legitimating narrative of the divine right of kings conferred by God through the church. This new story about the legitimacy of the people required new kinds of institutions and organizations to embody itself in a society. The result was a fundamental change in the political institutions and governing forms, with the introduction of institutions and structures such as regular elections and representative parliaments. While we now take these structures for granted, they had to be created out of fundamental changes in a society's stories about what was central to its identity and way of life. Behind most of our structures lie such legitimating narratives, stories about what a group believes most deeply express its beliefs, habits and practices.

What was so different about the denominational meeting described at the beginning of this chapter was that not too long ago national denominational agencies were viewed as central and normative forms of church life. In that meeting the existing organizational structure of national, regional and local church bodies was still, formally, the norm. Reports were given, motions voted on and officers elected. In the formal meeting nobody challenged this established legitimating narrative. They met *as if* national and regional church bodies were still normative. In the coffee gatherings afterwards, however, something massively different was happening—*practically* these people were saying they had lost confidence in such structures; they'd lost faith in their capacity to embody the values, commitments and habits of these people. In recent conversations with leaders in mid-judicatory systems (e.g., executive presbyters, regional conference executives, bishops) oponions are increasingly expressed in terms of their unease over the ways in which the existent structures, institutions and forms of government they have inherited are no longer able to address the complex challenges facing congregations and their leaders. Somehow, usually without a clear sense of alternatives, the legitimating narratives of the church members at the mandated meeting, and of a growing number of national and regional leaders, have shifted in some profound ways.

Changing legitimating narratives. This idea of a change in, or the erosion of, legitimating stories that once represented the core norms of a group or society is not limited to the churches but reaches into many of the legitimating narratives that have informed how our society has worked. The impasse and malaise, for example, observed in national and state governments polarized by ideologies has resulted in a deepening sense that government has little capacity to address the multiple crises in society, education, economics and the environment. When a rising percentage of citizens come to this conclusion, existing forms of political life are losing their legitimacy. This means that a growing percentage of people no longer believe the proposals and claims of existing parties are capable of addressing the challenges society faces. When this happens people begin to withdraw their trust in the stories and structures the parties operate within. Their legitimating narratives no longer compel people's loyalty or commitment.

The Occupy movement's demonstrations that began in fall 2011 outside the Wall Street Stock Exchange in New York spread across the

United States and spilled over to other Western states. It demonstrated how, after 2008/9, reigning economic narratives were losing their power of explanation for growing numbers of citizens. Something of profound importance was occurring, even if the actual protests and encampments lasted only a short while. The Occupy movement was the tip of an iceberg, beneath which growing numbers of ordinary citizens, who will not demonstrate, sense that the reigning economic story no longer serves them. What is at stake, what is being questioned, are these established, assumed legitimating narratives. Merely addressing the organizational structures (e.g., banking codes) without addressing these underlying narratives will bring short-term change that eventually returns things to the status quo. That is certainly the conclusion that many have reached about changes made to the banking system since 2008/9.[1]

LEGITIMATING NARRATIVES AND THE CHURCHES

The Eurotribal denominations are losing their capacity to provide meaning in our culture. In the minds of both those attending churches and the growing number opting out, the denominations have lost their legitimacy. Their institutions and structures were largely born out of periods of European and North American social history more and more remote to people's experience. That being said, structures are not willy-nilly add-ons that can be sloughed off when not needed. They are the concretization and expression of long-established and deeply held stories. Those regional-level denominational meetings are still shaped by the structures of denominational life, even while its leaders and members struggle with new questions about the value and role of the institutions that once served them well. Over time, structures change and institutions do get transformed, but such change emerges out of a period of wrestling with these deeper changes in legitimating narratives. Institutions don't usually start addressing the change issues they are facing by reflecting on their underlying narratives. The normative cycle is that denominations (even congregations) first respond to their changed contexts by developing processes of restructuring, revisioning or reprogramming. As one denominational leader recently observed, the past forty or more years have been one long period of trying out one "re-" plan after another. There is now a growing tiredness toward these initiatives. People are feeling like they have worked hard to fix the system but nothing has stuck. Another denominational leader described this as the new malaise that is characterizing conversation in denominations and, to some extent, congregations. This is actually a good moment. It signals that these systems may well be entering a space where they are ready to ask more critical questions about existing legitimating narratives.

Change does happen in legitimating narratives, and systems either adapt or die. Congregations and denominations can, and do, enter new periods of vitality and mission. We no longer, for example, build cathedrals. In large part because we're no longer a theocentric society that believes the cathedral expresses or embodies our deepest stories or values as a society (the legitimating narrative). We build banks, stock exchanges, shopping malls, sports stadiums and huge theaters to concretize some of our core legitimating narratives. Few believe, today, that the high-rise is the optimal way to thrive. As we grasp this relationship between structures and legitimating narratives, we can helpfully explore avenues for answering the question of how churches can engage the changed situation of the West. We're living in a tumultuous period when many existing legitimating stories are being challenged and upended. The challenge facing the Eurotribal denominations, including those movements that have sprung from them, is to understand how and why their once-persuasive legitimating narratives are being questioned. This will assist them in assessing what ways their structures and institutions may need to be remade, reclaimed, renewed, changed or abandoned.

Times of transition are confusing. We are in a time and space where so much is changing so quickly. Work is an example. Until recently most of us could count on keeping the job for which we were trained for a long time, if not all our working life. Today, most youth entering the work force will move through five to eight different jobs by the time they reach their late thirties, needing to retrain themselves several times along the way. What causes one social system to end and another to emerge? It is incredibly difficult to answer that question. It is clear, however, that understanding and learning how to address changes in legitimating narratives is a vital key to getting at how churches reimagine themselves. There is a lot going on here.

Passover and revolution. A powerful example of a legitimating narrative that makes sense of a group's identity (origins/sources) and gives it direction (defines what is important and what isn't) is the Passover feast rehearsed every year by Jewish communities. The Passover meal begins with a ritualized question that has been asked for millennia: "Why is this night different from all other nights?" The source of the question goes all the way back to the exodus:

> And when your children ask you, "What do you mean by this observance?" you shall say, "It is the passover sacrifice to the LORD, for he passed over the houses of the Israelites in Egypt, when he struck down the Egyptians but spared our houses. . . .
>
> You shall tell your child on that day, "It is because of what the Lord did for me when I came out of Egypt." (Ex 12:26-13:8)

This formative story (legitimating narrative), institutionalized in the yearly ritual practice, addresses the question of what it means to be a Jew. The story embedded in the practice makes sense of their origins, giving purpose and direction. It is a critical story that legitimates them as a people. But note how this deep, underlying story is given structure and is institutionalized in specific rituals that continually point this people back, behind themselves, to this formative story. Within the ritual structures the narrative is continually rehearsed, shaping generation after generation. It is a legitimating narrative. In a somewhat similar way, the founding stories of the American colonies and their Revolutionary War with England are deeply embedded in the collective memory of the American people. These stories continue to shape their identity, framing a sense of purpose and direction built into their Constitution and therefore embodied in political and social structures. Passover and revolution are deep, compelling stories. It's hard to imagine how they could lose their power to shape the lives of those indwelling them. Not all legitimating narratives are that large or compelling, but nonetheless they can have a profound influence on our lives. The Eurotribal denomina-

tions have exerted that kind of influence, but today they don't hold people's imagination in the same way.

In a recent book, *People of the Way*, theologian and missiologist Dwight
Zscheile traces the formation of a primary legitimating narrative among
Anglicans/Episcopalians from colonization of the Americas right into the
later part of the last century.[2] He describes this narrative as one of establishment: "Episcopalians have a particularly deep establishment legacy
that shapes our churches."[3] This legitimating narrative had its roots in
England, where Anglicanism was the national church. Early colonization
carried with it this assumed integration of church and state with its concomitant notion of the church as the civilizing force in society. This establishment narrative "brought with it particular ways of organizing the
church that continue to shape Anglican life, including in America."
Zscheile describes the interrelationship between legitimating narrative
and structural formation in the following manner:

> All the territory was divided up into parishes and dioceses, each under the
> authority of a monarchical rector or bishop, just as the same geography
> was controlled by monarchical political rulers—the king or queen, then
> princes, dukes, etc., down to village squires. The division of territory into
> dioceses and parishes reflects the reshaping of Christianity in the context
> of the Roman Empire (a diocese is a unit of Roman imperial governance).
> The church was positioned at the center, in a place of power and control.[4]

Zscheile points out that Christianity in its early period was shaped by
very different structures that reflected a very different narrative than that
of being at or near the centers of political and cultural power. In the
colonial period of the American story, Anglicanism was, for a time, the
official, established church of the Southern colonies. After the Revolution
this changed. While the Episcopal Church still imagined itself as the
established church, in the separation of church and state, this was no
longer the case in law. The shift that occurred was subtle but significant—
from *established church* to *church of the establishment*. In other words, the
underlying legitimating narrative remained that of establishment, with
all the accompanying structures this entailed. Zscheile says, "The Episcopal Church's self-confidence and social, cultural, and economic cen-

trality led to the articulation of the 'national church' ideal. . . . For an America growing in strength and power, the Episcopal Church was seen to offer a kind of *de facto* national church."[5] This establishment DNA has remained the underlying narrative framing the ethos, structures and imagination of the church, even while articulating strongly an advocacy for the outsider. The challenge for this denomination is that this legitimating narrative no longer engages or holds for people even while its structures continue to express and embody it.

STRUCTURES AND LEGITIMATING NARRATIVES

Structures, then, are how legitimating narratives are given material expression in organizations, groups and societies. We are embodied, meaning-making social beings who create structures to carry the stories that mold and define our lives. We are continually creating, living in and then discarding structures as the narratives that give meaning to our lives at particular times and in particular places shift and change. This meaning-making is complex. There isn't a simple, clear, neat, logical line from a legitimating narrative to a structure. The structures we live in are the result of continuous interactions with other stories and traditions. Structures are shaped through a continued process of negotiation amid the complex interactions between groups and across stories in everyday life. This negotiating is going on all the time. A magazine arrives at the door. Its headlines announce that a growing percentage of North Americans no longer live in families but are alone and are single. Why then, the front cover asks, are we still shaped by social structures designed for families? We pause to reflect and almost imperceptibly begin a process of renegotiation around legitimating narratives we've assumed to be normal. The Occupy movement raised questions about the ways we are making decisions about what is important as a society. It confronted us with new questions about the economic and political structures shaping our lives. This raising of questions subtly prods some of us to quietly renegotiate taken-for-granted assumptions about the economic and political structures we live in.

Such wrestling and renegotiating is going on all the time, but it's usually happening in the background in quiet, incremental ways. Changes in family demographics, for example, have been occurring gradually over several generations. Only quite recently have the implications of this huge shift in the way we live started to raise new questions about the kinds of structures we need to create to take in these changes. If a preponderance of social structures we have created are shaped to meet the needs of families (mom, dad and 2.5 kids), the new majority of singles find these structures alien to their experience. New questions are raised that challenge taken-for-granted assumptions: "What does belonging mean?" "Are structures designed around the family (e.g., single-family homes) sufficient to allow the new narrative to flourish?" "Does family mean male and female parents?" and so on.

Congregations, to continue the example, have been mostly designed around notions of the nuclear family. Such assumptions are now being renegotiated as this legitimating narrative of "family," which has shaped the structure of church life, has changed over the past several decades.

In the midst of these multiple, pervasive changes in North American culture, denominations are having a hard time figuring out how to adjust and reorient themselves. Generally, the structures and institutions of these denominations are in crisis. They no longer hold people's loyalty or commitment. But structure and institution in some form are critical for human thriving. Embodied, structured beings is what we are. Our skeletal structure provides the form for our embodied life; our skin is a living, structured organism that communicates with the world so we can structure responses to our environment. The embodied life we live is only possible as a function of the ways our bodies are structured. In a similar way, we're born into social institutions that structure much of how we act and perceive our world and ourselves even while we're shaped by stories and truths that invite us to question and at times change these structures. The family (now in its multitudinous forms) is a structure that embodies deep, even biological, narratives about how we thrive as human beings and how we regenerate ourselves. The challenge to multiple organizations and institutions, given this new majority of singles, is how to structure belonging and nurture social life when a specific legitimating narrative around family (the industrialized, nuclear family) is no longer a narrative in which a growing majority lives.

The earth's atmosphere, with its interrelationships of oceans, land-masses, gravitational fields and so forth, is a structured, living system. One of the arguments underlying the environmental movement is the need for us to recognize that our earth, in its complex interrelationships, is structured in quite specific ways. We can no longer view it as some neutral piece of matter we use for whatever ends we choose (a legitimating narrative that has provided a way of understanding and using the environment). Environmentalists argue that human activity over the past century has failed to recognize the intricate structuring of our planet. The result is that forms of natural life that have existed for millennia are now being torn apart. A legitimating narrative that proposed the earth to be little more than raw materials to be used at will through technological innovations has resulted in structures and organized ways of life that now appear to be unsustainable. Even as evidence piles up that human beings are causing the current global warming, governments at many levels fail to act with the level of direction that is needed. In North America, for example, there has been a precipitous decline in bee populations. Bees, by any accounting, are critical to food supplies and therefore a huge part of the economy. It is now evident that a certain set of pesticides are responsible for the decimation of bee populations, but there is little desire on the part of the Canadian government to act in ways that limit, or end, the use of pesticides that are now clearly as bad as DDT. Why? Because, as this government has made clear in other debates around global warming (the Alberta tar sands is an example), the short-term economy will always trump environmental issues. This is an issue of narratives. The modern, free-market economy is a more powerful shaping legitimating narrative for this government than the question of our relationship to creation.

Structures and organizational forms provide pathways and habits within which to live together. Once in place they can't be sloughed off, even when we conclude they need to change. I write this chapter sitting inside a long tube high above the Atlantic Ocean heading for the United Kingdom. What gets me across the Atlantic alive is a complex, sophisticated set of organizational structures, from the engineering of aircraft to the protocols of international aviation, from radar guidance systems to the explicit ways pilots are trained and graduate through a well-framed set of proficiency levels, right up to the airfields with all their coded lights and control towers. This highly complex set of structures is now essential to how we function as a society. They've become habituated expressions of underlying values and practices. Given the power of structures to shape our lives in so many diverse ways, a question arises: Why, at this time, do so many perceive the structures that have enabled North American society to thrive (including the churches) as less and less capable of carrying our stories about what is important and how life ought to work?

A GROWING DESIRE TO JETTISON STRUCTURES

An understandable dynamic in all this disruption is a drive to eradicate, change or renew denominational and congregational structures. This chapter has argued, however, that structures are in themselves a symptom, not the cause, of the current malaise. What we have observed over the past several decades has been this drive to problematize structures and institutions as the basic cause for the malaise. This focus assumes that removing or changing structures will address the challenges facing the churches. An unaddressed assumption in this is that structures are secondary, nonessential accretions (like barnacles) that obscure the true, essential church from breaking forth.

A massive sea change in people's perspectives about denominations and congregations has been occurring over the last half century. Church structures have gone from being viewed as critical, positive elements of social life to an element that thwarts, squashes, undermines and confines the church. Similar shifts are taking place in the political, economic and educational realms. Structures that formed generations of citizens, giving them a sense of place and purpose, have gone from being seen as essential underpinnings of social life to mechanisms used by power elites or regressive bureaucracies to control and thwart human thriving. This is a huge change in legitimating narratives.

What is happening? Is it as simple as existing structures being worn out and needing to be replaced? Some of this erosion of confidence in dominant structures is a response to a pervasive sense of loss across our society.[6] Another part is people's awareness of finding themselves in a place where they have never been before, where the maps that once made sense of their world no longer describe their current reality. When such disruptions happen, we look for explanations that fit our existing maps. The temptation is to view existing structures as the primary issue. On this basis there are continual moves to remake structures. While this will need to happen, it's a question of the basis for remaking, renewing or reclaiming structures. What has to happen first is to understand where, why and how the underlying stories and narratives that resource these structures have changed. An examination of the numerous attempts at restructuring and reorganizing that have been a prevalent part of the church landscape for almost half a century will show that little in these efforts have affected any change in the unraveling. The malaise has continued to deepen. The experience of organizational and structural changes for most denominations and congregations has been a brief period of energy and reduced anxiety, only to be replaced by a return to the unraveling and the malaise.

The reasons for this will be given extended treatment later in the book. An example, however, of how denominations have operated is given here. The dominant form of organizational life shaping denominations is the *corporate* denomination. Built along the model of the twentieth-century corporations, with head offices, regional centers and end-user customers, these were institutions shaped by a specific story of how to get effective results. In brief, these organizations gathered experts and professionals in a wide variety of areas into a central hub from which they designed programs, created strategic plans and disseminated their resources, products and programs to their regional distribution centers, and from there to the end users (congregations). This organizational structure is characterized by assumptions about how to manage a system successfully. Strategic planning, for example, was one of its primary tools.[7] In this way of planning, experts gathered data, studied the various elements of a situation, and identified the gap between where they were and where they wanted to be at a point in the future. On this basis a plan was developed to get from one point to the next. This form of planning has been the primary imagination within denominational systems, and despite the adoption of different language, its basic assumptions still determine much of their planning activity. This kind of imagination still drives their reorganizing and restructuring efforts. While leaders in these systems grasp that there are huge shifts occurring in the culture and that church systems are failing to engage them, the explanations and answers being provided remain inside existing maps and the application of existing skills. But the unraveling is creating a situation where these maps no longer read the world we've entered, so planning processes recommending organizational and structural change will probably misdirect. A different approach is needed. New spaces can't be managed with existing skills. This is why changing structures won't get at the issue of how an organizational system (such as a denomination or local church) engages a new space, even if doing these things reduces the anxiety of those in charge.

What perspectives do we need to address this critical question of structures and their role in the midst of a great unraveling? Are they simply the tools power elites use to control and manipulate the unsuspecting masses? Do they represent the last throes of dinosauric institutions and leaders trying to hold on to an untenable past, staunching the cracks before the tsunami of postmodernity? Are structures merely like the pipes a plumber puts in the walls of a house—necessary but blessedly hidden, out of the way because they're just there to help get the real work done? Or are structures something else altogether? Are existing structures (the old, outdated plumbing, to continue the metaphor) to be pulled out of the house (the old soldered joints are leaking, the U-traps plugged and the copper lines thinning and ready to burst), merely old materials to be discarded and replaced with a whole new set of structures? Or is there something much more significant and essential about structures missed in this apposition between *old* and *new*, *then* and *now*? What frameworks and resources do we need to address these critical questions?

Structure and Institutions

The institutions we construct and the values they espouse and promulgate are closely related to the cultural imaginary.

Graham Ward, *The Politics of Discipleship*

The key, it becomes evermore apparent, lies with institutions. . . . [Institutions] are, of course, in some sense the products of culture. . . . Because they formalize a set of norms, institutions are often the things that keep a culture honest.

Niall Ferguson, *Civilization: The West and the Rest*

INSTITUTIONAL STRUCTURES: MEANING AND ROLE

Niall Ferguson's *Civilization* proposes a set of factors (the "killer apps") that created the single most important phenomenon of the past five centuries, namely, the ascent and dominance of the West. One of Ferguson's core convictions is that the institutional structures developed by the West provide the clues to its ability to thrive and transform the rest of the world. At the same time, Ferguson articulates an anxiety felt by many in the West in the early decades of the new millennium. He owns that at some point in the first decades of this century it hit him that "we are living through the end of 500 years of Western ascendancy."[1]

This anxiety is keenly felt across the West. It has become the backdrop

to a continual handwringing around questions of what has gone wrong
and what might be done to turn the tide. Postmortems are premature
and unwarranted. What is clear, however, is that this anxiety causes
many Westerners to write off the ways of life, forms, structures and institutions that have given the Western project its energy. Similarly, there
are those who pronounce eulogies over the Eurotribal churches. Anxiety
over the state of these churches has produced a myriad of calls for the
creation of a new kind of church. There seems to be a regular stream of
proposals for some new form of church, together with plans and strategies to arrive in some new place as quickly as possible. A few illustrations can only indicate the growing length of these proposals: *sticky*
church, *emergent* church, *fresh expressions* church, *simple* church, *new
parish* churches, *missional* churches, *organic* church and so on. The point
here is not to critique the content of these proposals but to suggest that
this growing list of proposals, like Ferguson's own confession, is an
anxious realization that something is wrong. Some proposals dig back
into what they perceive as some biblical norm for order (e.g., the so-
called fivefold ministry of Ephesians 4), suggesting that part of the solution is to replace the prominence of the pastor-teacher role in favor of
some new kind of apostolic order. None of this comes close to what is
at stake. While we are all (not just the churches) in uncharted spaces of
disruption, Ferguson's caution about simply throwing out the institutions and structures that formed Western life is worthy of some pause
before racing off into the brave new world of change. Two authors who
might assist us in pausing to reflect and discern are Pierre Bourdieu and
Graham Ward.

BOURDIEU AND HABITUS

Pierre Bourdieu (1930-2002) was a leading sociologist and philosopher
who argued that ways of life, in practices and habits, are internalized
deep within us and expressed in institutions. We are shaped by our participation in a social community and its patterns of life (including organizational structures) that is itself rooted in history and tradition. His
language for this complex shaping of our living is *habitus*. The term refers
to the histories and traditions we are embedded in that reach back into

a long past and are not dead. Rather, they are very much alive and are being expressed in and through us as members of social communities, institutions and organizations. As such, we cannot simply cast off our institutions and structures like some external garment, or pull them out like old plumbing (this was the terrible mistake of two of the three great ideological revolutions of modernity—the French and Russian).[2] The radical overthrow of deeply embedded ways of life results in profoundly destructive consequences for the great masses of ordinary people caught in the ideologies of change. This is not an argument for stasis or a passive acceptance of what exists, but a caution about believing too quickly the claims of those who say existing institutional structures are moribund and therefore need to be excised for the sake of something new.

We are embedded in a complex set of narratives that have become structured in our habits and ways of life. The liturgies and rituals of a family, government, bike gang or denomination shape their members in taken-for-granted ways of life. Bourdieu used the word *habitus* to describe these habits, practices, histories and ways of life. It is a concept for understanding how social groups function. Social structures are produced and reproduced through an underlying habitus. As a product of history, the habitus produces individual and social practices embedded in organizations such as families, parliaments, denominations and congregations in accordance with traditions that continually reactivate themselves in structured practices. A more popular, albeit inadequate, way of describing this is to speak of our defaults. What Bourdieu helps us to see is that institutional structures are more than external skin; they go deep into the nature of who we are as a society, group or system. Simply assuming we can discard them like the clothes we wear is naive. It's like believing shaving hair off the skin ends the dynamics that produce the hair in the first place.

The habitus of a group or organization is not consciously mastered and changed, as if it were some objectified thing that can be worked on and manipulated to one's preferred ends. The habitus of a system runs far deeper; it outruns people's conscious intentions to simply make institutional and structural change in the name of some planned future. This is why changing structures usually doesn't substantively change much of anything. Across multiple denominational systems in numerous countries I have led the leaders of these systems through processes where they have named all the change initiatives they've worked on for the past decade of more. Some of these lists get quite long, with one national denomination able to name some seventeen such initiatives. The majority of them are in the form of restructuring and reorganizing their systems. In each case these leaders come to the same conclusion—the restructuring and reorganizing has not changed the overall loss of identity of the denomination or church.

Changing structures, in and of itself, doesn't address the habitus of a congregation or denomination. This is why restructuring and reorganizing processes in denominations and congregations leave them looking much like what they sought to replace. Defaults go deep. They reassert themselves despite the best-intended organizational change and strategic planning. This does not mean organizational systems must continually repeat their past. It doesn't mean they are unchangeable. The transformation of social systems, however, is not primarily a function of changed structures or institutions. It is about how a social community discerns and learns those habits and practices that assist it to thrive. This is time-consuming work.

GRAHAM WARD AND IMAGINARIES

Graham Ward, a theologian at the University of Manchester, uses the language of "social" or "cultural imaginary." This language of cultural imaginary is new for many.[3] It's connected, as the language suggests, with the idea of imagination. Simply put, the social imaginary of a group consists of the narratives (the stories that give meaning to how it came into being, why it exists, etc.) and practices that shape its common life. A group, such as a congregation or a denominational system, doesn't spend a lot of time reflecting on the language and stories they use to describe themselves or their relationship to the surrounding culture. But for a while try becoming a part of a worshiping community that is outside your experience and see if you don't, initially, sense that these people have ways of doing things and using language that are unfamiliar to you but taken-for-granted by them. They will use words in ways that seem quite strange initially and talk to one another as if everyone knows what they mean. In one congregation people will walk into the *sanctuary* (for other groups it's an *auditorium*, and for others it's a *worship center*), dip their fingers in a font of water and use it to make the sign of the cross; another group will move to the church's center aisle, turn toward the front, bend forward and cross themselves; still another group will head for the coffee pot and immediately begin conversations, while yet another will sit quietly in a pew, bow their heads and pray. Each is a form of entering shaped by a different social imaginary.

The language we use, the stories we tell and the practices we repeat each time we enter a church building or attend a denominational meeting continually shape how a group behaves. Language and practices are the vehicles for continually forming a group's imaginary—its way of being in a place. Some church groups, for example, refer to each other as "brothers" and "sisters"; others find words like *issues* to be red flags that put the group in conflict with one another. Some denominations have embodied practices that express how they imagine their deepest convictions about life. Communion, for example, expresses a whole way of believing that is embodied around a liturgy and a table. For other church groups this is called the "Lord's Supper," and in that different descriptor for the same event (externally) there lies a very different imagination for what the event is about. In yet other church systems the language used is "Eucharist," and again under the word lies another imagination for what, outwardly, looks like the same activity. Each language form embodies a different imagination about what these words mean and how they are practiced.

For Ward, the idea of cultural imaginary is a way of describing how we structure and live the way we do in a particular social group at a particular time. Any social group, whether a northern England pub crowd or Deep South golf club of the United States, whether a group of biker gangs gathering in Colorado Springs for a weekend or a community of Goths in Oxford, has a set of interacting stories, rituals and ways of talking (language houses) that continually intermix to form how that group, as a group, sees the world and acts together. The biker clubs and the Goths, for example, would behave in very different ways if they both had a weekend meeting in Colorado Springs at the same time. Each would look at the other recognizing that they lived in different worlds with different comprehensions, practices and stories about themselves and the other. In other words, they each live in a cultural imagination (imaginary) formed over time through their interactions with one another and the larger social environment. If we could participate in these groups for a time, we'd recognize different ways of talking, different kinds of practices and a variety of stories that give them their identity as a group. These stories and ways of framing their worlds shape how they act together as a group (their structures and institutions).

In this sense the cultural imaginaries we live within (a denominational tradition, a singing group, soccer club or international corporation such as Apple, Google or General Motors) shape how we organize, structure and institutionalize our worlds as a community.[4] As Graham Ward suggests, "Our ideas are formed out of the molten core of imagined possibilities that the cultures we inhabit furnish. This imaginary opens a space for what is possible. From these possibilities new institutions arise."[5] Thus, the imaginary that informs a biker club is patently different from that which forms a Goth club. The obvious markers of these different cultural imaginaries are in the dress codes each takes on, the ways they structure and organize their groups, and the instruments they use. Ward's point is that these imaginaries are formed out of a mixture, a flux of stories, images, histories and so on that are present as possibilities for each group. Out of this flux, this molten core of possibilities, each group creates structures and institutions to demarcate and order their lives. A casual observation of both groups will indicate ornate internal practices, structures and institutionalizations that shape certain convictions about themselves and the world.

IMAGINARIES, CHANGE AND STRUCTURES

Structures and institutions are the concretization, the ritualization, of these deeper, preconscious imaginaries. Institutions and structures are not just made up like some extraneous cloth draped over a painting. They are expressions of embedded and deeply held cultural imaginaries. What is happening in periods of profound change, such as our own, is that these preconscious social imaginaries are being challenged, even undermined. People start to feel that their basic structuring of meaning is no longer making sense of their experience, and so they start to question long-held practices and social relationships. Practices developed over generations no longer result in expected, habitual outcomes. Underlying, long-established narratives are then called into question. But cultural imaginaries are hardly ever clearly articulated or consciously owned views of how the world works. They lie under the surface at a taken-for-granted, precritical level of our social life.

Not until these are brought to the surface, until people become aware of their operative power, can a group realistically understand what is happening to them. Only out of that understanding can they evaluate in any meaningful way what the transformations in the context are going to mean for them as a group. Even at that point, proposing wholesale change is misguided. Groups slough off their past as nothing, to their own detriment. What is required is not the deconstruction of structures or even the restructuring or reengineering of organizations. Proposals for new structures to displace old traditional or institutional systems deflect energy away from process that would invite people to discover what underlying issues of change might be. *What a group needs is not primarily a new restructuring proposal but time and ways in which they can learn to name and test new habits and practices in the new space.*

As counterintuitive as this may sound, the focus of energy in an organization should not be placed on proposals for organizational change but on inviting people into some initially simple places where they can experiment in new habits and practices. One denomination, for example, had gone through a series of restructuring processes for a decade. A great deal of institutional energy and resources had been given to these efforts, but the general consensus had changed little. People's confidence in these approaches was very low. A suspicion of and resistance to further such denominational changes was emerging. What we recommended was that they not enter into additional programs but instead invite people into a series of experiments around what congregations and regional leaders were naming as the core challenges they were facing (e.g., How does a congregation reconnect with its neighborhoods? How does a midlevel judicatory discover how to form the kinds of leaders it needs at this point in time? How do we reconnect with youth?). Learning experiments were created across the system to work on these questions. In doing so, congregations, clergy, regional leaders and, to some extent, national leaders started to name some of the underlying narratives, assumptions and defaults that were shaping their actions. They started to recognize how these attitudes and values were embedded in structures and organizational forms that might have become barriers to engaging neighborhoods or connecting with youth or forming new kinds of leaders. Out of such experiments people's awareness of their narratives became the primary learning.

While these processes took time, as people experimented they learned there was a lot of common energy among them; they learned to take risks together. All of this started to create a new kind of space where people could begin asking different questions about their structures. Such experiments make it possible for organizations to then reenter their tradition and history in order to reframe their life in a new space. At this juncture organizational and institutional change is effective. This is not an easy journey, because it tends to be counterintuitive to the ways leaders have generally functioned. What follows are some examples of the defaults that tend to push denominational leaders in the direction of organizational and institutional changes as the solution to the crises their systems face.

THE "OLD" VERSUS "NEW," "SPIRIT" VERSUS "STRUCTURE" FAIRY TALE

The ideas of *structure* and *institution*, their meaning, place and role, have undergone profound transformations in the latter half of the twentieth century. Once respected words in our lexicon, they've fallen into disrepute. This is reflected in ways the language of "structure" has come under suspicion among newer movements of church transformation, which argue we live in a postmodern space where the structures and institutions of modernity no longer have validity and therefore need to be jettisoned. An underlying imaginary driving this argument is the notion of progress. The idea of progress lies at the imaginative core of modernity. Its narrative myth assumes that the past is to be overcome to make way for the new, a future which is, by definition, always better.

This perspective appears in numerous forms. Often framed as a juxta-position between *old* and *new*, the myth goes something like this: We, the enlightened, perceive the new in the postmodern world emerging before us while the traditionalists seek to defend the old ways of doing things. David Harvey describes this as the "fairy-tale reading of the difference between the 'then' and the 'now.'" For Harvey, this fairy tale damages our ability to see what is actually happening around us, especially in times of disruptive change when any kind of myth is eagerly embraced if it promises the end of anxiety.[6] This hegemonic (totalizing) concept of progress assumes an either-or opposition between *then* (modernity, Christendom or traditional structures) and *now* (the so-called emerging, organic, natural or postmodern world). Based on this polarity people are invited to presume that in our postmodern space we have entered such a new era that we are now part of the new time (referred to as the *kairos* moment). Much of this narrative is part of a yet deeper social imaginary based in notions of the self-making, self-authenticating individual and notions of expressive individualism. There is something very beguiling about this imaginary—to be told that our time is the time of the new. It also betrays how superficial and self-serving postmodern language can be. The basis of this narrative is actually modernity itself.

New leaders and movements are, by implication, distinguished from their immediate predecessors, and are unwilling to jettison existing structures, thus making their predecessors part of the disposable past (a sign of a totalitarian myth is the way it objectifies in order to dispose the other who fails to get with the program). The notion of structures has fallen victim to this newspeak, observed, for example, in the juxta-position of the idea of "structure" with that of "emergence," wherein structure is an old concept that must give way to the new. Such romantic ideology bears no relationship to the world in which we live our everyday lives. In this newspeak *organic* functions like a magic wand mysteriously ushering us into the new, postmodern; whereas *structure* functions like some inhibiting old, reactive force. Inside this neat polarity, structures and institutions that have shaped the churches are neatly wiped away. But be attentive to what is happening. Cultural imaginaries are operative;

models of the mind are predetermining how the world is read. The language of "emergent," "organic" and "new" forms a potent mix that beguiles people in anxious systems into the latest fashion and fads in the age-old myth that jettisoning the old and embracing the new fixes the problem. If only it were so.

In a time of a massive unraveling, it is helpful to remind ourselves of other, earlier moments of upheaval when questions of structure were wrestled over. Following the birth of Pentecostalism, at the beginning of the twentieth century, there were those enthused by the Spirit who declared the emergence of a whole new era, a new time which would remove the need for what was perceived as the life-denying structures of the existing churches. The same mythical ideology is still present in current conversations about missional life, where some write and speak about so-called emergent structures. Within these narratives lurks the perspective that existing structures are the problem, and the solution is simply to discard them because they are deemed irrelevant. These arguments are not new but actually repeat well-established patterns.

It is easy to fall prey to the fairy tale of the *then* and *now*, and be deflected from struggling with deeper questions of how the Spirit might seek to reshape traditions in fresh ways. Even this question of discerning the work of the Spirit is often placed inside the mythical polarity of Spirit versus structure. Even the best minds can be shaped by this polarity. It is fascinating to read Jaroslav Pelikan's description of the church some five hundred years ago. It might have been written today.

> The institutions of . . . Christendom [were] in trouble, and everyone knew it. Intended as windows through which men might catch a glimpse of the Eternal, they became opaque, so that the faithful looked at them rather than through them. The structures of the church were supposed to act as vehicles of the spirit—both for the Spirit of God and the spirit of man. Here the Christian believer was to find, in an available and indeed palpable form, the very grace of God. Instead, what he found was a distortion of the faith . . . in fact, a whole series of obstacles to the authentic life of the human spirit and to the activity of the Holy Spirit. Captive in ecclesiastical structures that no longer served as channels of divine life and means of divine grace, the spiritual power of the Christian gospel pressed to be released.[7]

A new majority of Christians echo Pelikan's beautifully balanced words, taken from the first chapter of his 1968 book on Luther and the Reformation. Their sentiment is repeated often today in the form of a critique of existing church structures. Vehicles formed to express our deepest convictions about how to live as Christians in the world are increasingly experienced as barriers to and distortions of the life of God. Structures that once gave life to Christian imagination are experienced as impediments.

It is certainly true that a growing majority of Christians in Western societies no longer find in existing church structures windows through which they can glimpse the Spirit of God or express their own spiritual yearnings. These voices conclude that current structures, inherited from the twentieth century or accreted since the Reformation, are no longer viable. There is truth in such claims. Without question, something needs to be done about the crisis of the churches![8] Before defaulting, however, to a "then" and "now" or "spirit–structure" solution, we should inquire a little more into what is actually causing these structures to be viewed as barriers to the Spirit. Is it the case that the Spirit of God is being thwarted primarily by the structures, or is something else going on? Why is there such incredulity toward many forms of structured social life at this time (not just in the church but beyond)? It's not just the churches that have lost the trust and confidence of people. Something broader and more pervasive is going on. What are the underlying reasons for this more general loss of confidence in these particular structures? Why are growing numbers of people across all kinds of systems losing confidence in structures that until very recently mediated meaning, shaped practices, formed habits and enabled people in the West to thrive?

These critical questions need attention. Beneath them lie other even more troubling issues. There is a pervasive anxiety that the core narratives of Western culture have eroded. Those committed to the Christian narrative recognize that it is ever more difficult to pass the tradition on. How might we shape our faith so that it will still hold the imagination and commitment of people in the West? More than forty years ago Lesslie Newbigin framed this concern in the form of a question: "What would be involved in a genuinely missionary encounter between the gospel and the culture that is shared by the peoples of Europe and North America, their colonial and cultural off-shoots, and the growing company of educated leaders in the cities of the world?"[9] In less prosaic words: Will our children have faith? Even more pointedly: Will the faith have our children? At this point it doesn't look promising! If the primary response to these deeper, pervasive anxieties is the drive to dispose of existing structures and replace them with new ones, we will be continually misdirected from the critical work of addressing the underlying narratives.

Structures mediate meaning. For a significant period of time denominational and congregational structures effectively mediated cultural meaning for large numbers of people. Until quite recently these structures concretized the narratives and social imaginaries of a significant percentage of people in North America. They were the embodiment, brick, sinew and roadway of social meanings built over generations and carried forward by generations. They framed for people their identity and located them within a larger cultural narrative. Structures that shaped generations, providing meaning and identity to whole cultures are not easily dismissed.

TRANSFORMATION EMERGES FROM HABITS AND PRACTICES

The Christian narrative is rooted and founded in the gospel, which is always borne with some kind of tradition. The gospel as a narrative story comes through generations of transmission. This transmission is continually embedded practices (the Eucharist is one such example of such a practice, as are the various liturgies of churches). At the same time the gospel and the practices that make it contemporary for us are continually being institutionalized and structured into our everyday life. No narrative survives without this transmission over time. The result is a complex, intricate commingling of the narrative, its practices and institutions that taken together shape a people's identity. Membership in a group with its ritualized procedures enables us to carry forward the life of our tradition. Institutions and structures are an essential part of this. This is why in times of rapid social change and the loss of confidence in legitimating narratives, a primary focus in institutional change is insufficient.

At the core of the challenges confronting the Eurotribal churches is the question of the transmission of the gospel into this transforming Western society (Newbigin's question is cited earlier). As throughout the church's history, we are continually concretizing the gospel in institutional structures. Ours is one of those times when the institutions and structures that have sustained our narratives are being questioned. We need to resist the temptation to simply change structures in order to understand what is at stake in terms of this gospel engagement with our changing culture. This is not to deny the need for structural and institutional change, but a question of the order in which we address these questions.

Because we all live inside some core narrative about how the world works and how we are to behave (social imaginary), we usually do not stop to ask why we structure the world or our systems in the ways we do. It's just how the world is! What is at stake is not primarily replacing structures but discerning the kinds of legitimating narratives that are being expressed in these structures.[10] The challenge is in discerning again how the gospel might engage a time of massive cultural change in order to address the question of the institutions and structures that might best enable us to carry this out at this moment in time.

Existing church structures are not inviolable and do not last forever. The current structures of Protestantism were formed inside the social imaginary of a generative period of Western Christian life (the various reformations of the fifteenth- and sixteenth-century Europe). We have to ask if the legitimating narratives that formed churches in this period, for example, or even in the first half of the twentieth century, can provide the basis for an engagement with our time.

Reevaluating
Structure and Spirit

INTRODUCTION

The call for a revaluation of church structures and institutions is right.
Something about existing structures and institutions is amiss. The reality
of the situation can be heard in voices gone silent—the growing mass of
Christians leaving churches because the forms and structures no longer
sustain Christian life at this time.[1]

It takes little prescience to recognize that the structures of church life
in Protestant North America no longer serve as effective channels of
God's life. The power of the gospel seems lost in the iron cages of organizational systems and their bureaucratic hierarchies. These systems
seem ill-fitted to engage the profound changes reshaping our societies in
ways we still aren't able to comprehend.

One large mainline denomination, hemorrhaging membership and
endowment funds for several decades, turns its energies to rewriting
basic organizational and operating polity documents. These documents
describe the order and structures the church must operate within. Listening to leader after leader across that system, it is clear there is no
energy for this project. Those in the field, outside the inner circles of
national offices, recognize that these rewriting processes, despite best
intentions, simply don't come close to addressing the underlying issues
people sense but often can't name. These deeper challenges are about the
legitimating narratives that gave shape to structure and polity manuals

in the first place. The validity of these narratives is now under question. Denominations, despite their best theological statements and confessions, have lost touch with the massive cultural shifts reshaping Western societies. Such shifts are not primarily about structures; they're about narratives. Our narratives are about the stories we believe and around which we build our lives (e.g., we want to be a "gospel people" or a "kingdom people" or a "community of Jesus-followers"). These narratives get expressed in habits and practices that are usually embodied through institutions and structures.

Throughout the church's history voices have called out, echoing this sense that structures and institutions that once opened windows out onto the world and the movement of God have somehow closed, creating stifling environments that no longer mediate the life of God's people. We live in such a time. We also live within a long story of *semper reformanda* (the church is always being reformed). The echoes of this wrestling to always reform—from forefathers and foremothers in each of our traditions—reverberate again in our time. This tension between established, assumed structures, the sense that something is amiss and the search for structures that might again mediate the life of the Spirit is always a challenge for the church.

JERUSALEM: SPIRIT AND STRUCTURE

Recall the debates in the Jerusalem church right after Pentecost. So much of that sharp, divisive conflict was about the appropriate mediating structures, the language of "meaning," within which this young movement would be formed. There, structures expressed an established narrative of what it meant to be a follower of Jesus. Immediately after Pentecost the limits of the language this young movement indwelled shaped the groups' assumptions about the structures that would form them. For instance, they initially assumed it to be a temple-centered renewal movement within Judaism. Notice what was happening. Even with a high sense that something radically new had been birthed by the Spirit, their language world had already located this movement within existent structures of Judaism. If they'd remained within this language world (the existing legitimating narrative of an internal Jewish restoration movement), it would have limited their imagination and could not have mediated what the Spirit was going to do in the world. So, being emergent or postmodern or "Spirit-led" doesn't get one off the hook from the hard work of understanding the nature of structures and the ways our use of language functions inside structures that shape how we act.[2]

The legitimating narrative taken up immediately after Pentecost was centered in Jerusalem and embodied (structured and institutionalized) in temple-centered worship and specific dietary practices. These structures and practices quickly framed the character of the post-Pentecost community. Left in this structuring of their life, this young movement would have been shaped by an existent story about the nature of God and the locus of God's work (Jerusalem and Judaism) that would have turned the movement Jesus inaugurated into another sectarian subset of first-century Palestinian Judaism.

ACTS: SPIRIT AND STRUCTURE

The early chapters of Acts are filled with strife. On the surface the conflict appears to be about structures and institutions (e.g., What is the role of the dietary laws? What are the parameters for belonging? Who is allowed in and on what conditions? Where does authority reside?). But just beneath the surface of these structural and institutional tensions lie deeper questions about the nature of the basic story in which this young community will live. Luke deliberately depicts the Spirit in the role of continually breaking the boundaries of the existing Jerusalem imagination. This was not primarily a matter of old structures needing to give way to some new forms. More critically, it was a struggle to understand the kind of story they were living in. Simply disposing of structures and replacing them with different ones would not get at these more basic questions of the narratives the new community was to live by. Similar questions are at stake today in the North American church.

The drama of Acts reveals leaders (Paul, Peter, James and likely a host of others whose names are not recorded) in tension over the question of what was at stake. They engaged in the tension-riddled debate over the nature of the story, but in the end they weren't beguiled by the assumption this was merely a fight between old and new structures. The Jerusalem

Council itself was an ad hoc structure for engaging these important debates. These leaders understood that the story that shaped them would determine the structures they produced.

EPHESIANS: SPIRIT AND STRUCTURE

One place where this is exemplified is in Ephesians.[3] Paul is working through a practical theological discourse that seeks to understand the fundamental meaning of what God was doing in Christ. Its long, doxological prologue is a hymn of praise for what God has done in Jesus Christ from "before the foundation of the world" (Eph 1:4). In Paul's framing, God is the active agent, always the center of what is happening. What Paul is describing is, therefore, not an accident of history but the outworking of God's purposes. The center of this is expressed in Ephesians 1:9-11, where he declares that now, in Jesus Christ, the mystery hidden since before the foundation of the world has been revealed. In this Jesus, God is bringing back together, reconciling and healing into a doxological life the whole of creation. In these assertions Paul lives deeply within the story of his tradition, that story that is present through the Scriptures and at the same time is reworking the story in the light of the radical, new centering of all things in Jesus Christ. Given the new situation the resurrection has created, Paul wrestles with questions of what this means practically for these new communities shaped around the confession of Jesus as Lord and practices such as forms of gathering, Eucharist, table fellowship and leadership. In other words, he's working out what the structures and institutions of daily life need to look like.

Paul is wrestling with how this radically new narrative cuts through some of the deepest narratives of his time and human history. What does this new story mean for the relationships between Jews and Greeks, slave and free, women and men? The existent relationships among these polarities, the ways these relationships were structured in social life (social imaginaries), came from somewhere. They didn't just happen. They were the ways people had come to structure their deepest beliefs, their narrative stories about these relationships. What Paul now does is decenter existing stories, and in so doing invite the young church to imagine structures and ways of instituting social life that reflect the story of God's reconciling presence in Jesus Christ.

We observe Paul working with a series of metaphors that try to give expression to what these new structures and institutions might be. He uses the metaphor of a great wall being broken down so that all may now move into a new kind of space. That new space is described through multiple lenses (metaphors), none of which, in itself, expresses the whole picture. Foreigners become citizens; aliens are bound into a new family; the new space is like a house being built with many kinds of bricks, all bound together on the foundations of the traditions of God's movement through history (the prophets) and the radically new reality in Jesus Christ. The imagery morphs into metaphors of joints and ligaments knit together, organs and parts of difference operating in concert through Christ the head and the binding Spirit.

These pictures and descriptions represent the radically new story implicit in the long doxological introduction in Ephesians 1. They now have to find new ways of being embodied in structures and institutions that could concretize this new narrative. Part of what we observe in the Pauline epistles is how this young movement is testing, learning and discovering how to structure their everyday life around this transformative story. Structures and institutions were in flux. They were experimental. Tradition and innovation seemed to coexist in this space of learning and discovery. The basic structures of these new communities did not spring up *de novum* as some radical innovation that represented a fundamental break with the past. They were mostly borrowed from existing structural forms in the Greco-Roman culture of time. Household systems provided the language and forms for what later periods turned into hard and fast forms of life (presbyters, bishops and deacons). But the New Testament texts suggest communities were experimenting with the structures and institutions that were in their everyday lives as a means of forming this new story of God's movement in Jesus Christ in their time and place. They were figuring out forms on the way.

WHAT IS AT STAKE

The question about the role of structures in the life of the church is not a polarity between Spirit and structure, as if the Spirit gives life but structures deny the life of the Spirit. It is about what is at stake in the underlying narratives and how those narratives take form in the concrete contexts of everyday life. Luke-Acts and Ephesians demonstrate that the Spirit continually pushes the church, in its particular time and place, to reenter the story of Jesus Christ in order to wrestle with the question of how this narrative is given structure in terms of institutions and organizations. As the social and cultural contexts continue to change, the Spirit continually invites and empowers the church to discern the ways that its institutions and structures must be reshaped, reformed.

Bryan Stone expresses this reality in his study on evangelism after Christendom. He states that "one of the challenges of Christian evangelism today is that in order to learn to once again bear faithful witness to the Spirit's creative 'social work,' it may have to reject as heretical the pervasive characterization of salvation as a 'personal relationship with Jesus.'"[4] He suggests that a gospel understanding of evangelism often "runs counter to the social, political, and economic patterns narrated by modernity and enshrined in such 'imaginaries' as the individual, the nation-state, and the market."[5]

The disruptive Spirit is continually opening spaces that invite us to wrestle again with how our institutions and organizational structures will need to be changed in order for them to become again hopeful ways of shaping of Christian witness. In our time these structures have been formed, for example, out of notions of individual transactions (the gospel as a means of self-actualization or social contract) or nationalism (civil religion) or economic-consumer transactions (church as the consumption of religious goods and services by seekers). As with Paul's own wrestling with the structures of church life in Ephesians, the Spirit invites us to continually discern church structures that provide a means for gospel to disrupt accepted norms and narratives.

STRUCTURE, SPIRIT AND DISCERNMENT

Engaging our existing denominational and congregational structures in the light of the changed context of the Eurotribal churches is primarily a work of discernment. This is about a theological imagination of what

God is doing in our time. Whenever the theological imagination that perceives God as the active agent in the church and the world becomes secondary (at best), the church becomes stagnant and irrelevant.

Discernment invites practices of waiting before the Spirit in the midst of the unraveling occurring about us. The question of what kinds of organizational structures and institutions will best serve the Eurotribal churches in the space will come from this process of discerning the ways God's Spirit is at work in our contexts just now. Discernment in these matters is critical because we actually don't know what the road ahead looks like. This is why theological imagination and spiritual discernment are crucial. They are the prelude to and the means by which we will discern the organizational structures we need, because they move us in the direction of addressing our basic assumed narratives. Theological imagination and discernment invite us, first, to turn our attention toward the narrative memory of God's purposes. They invite a creative reentering of our stories and traditions.

Our particular traditions, our imagination around what God is about in our time and the current organizational structures we inhabit are all interconnected. Engaging them together is the key to innovation. Together they are the means by which we reenter the narrative world of God's story in Scripture as experienced through our particular traditions. Together, they are intricately interwoven means by which the Spirit both dislocates and reforms us as a people. Discernment and theological imagination invite all God's people; *all* God's people engage their traditions and their sense of the unraveling of the assumed stories that once seemed to work so well.

To declare that existing structures need to go into the garbage bin of history and be replaced with new ones is to assume implicitly that in making such a claim one stands in the privileged position of seeing the geography of the new space we have entered. That is a claim we would want to make very carefully.

While current church structures are less and less capable of mediating gospel life to increasing numbers of people, we need to resist the temptation of jumping too quickly to proposals for restructuring and reorganizing. Rather, we need to wrestle with questions of theological imagi-

66 2STRUCTURED FOR MISSION

nation and discernment such as: How might we go on a journey together
of discerning what the Spirit is doing ahead of us in our neighborhoods
and communities? How might we join with the Spirit in these places?
What are the appropriate practices of such joining?[6] What rhythms of life
undergird a theological discernment that assists people to develop
mission-shaped lives?[7] What is the relationship between the ways our
language describes how we see the world and the structures we create to
embody that way of seeing the world?

Most of us have inherited traditions that centuries ago framed an understanding of what God is about in the world within concrete structures.
We have tended to lose sight of the fact that those structures (e.g., the
presbytery form of church life developed by Calvin) were deeply influ-
enced by the philosophical, social and political assumptions of a period
in history. They were created by human beings who lived within a language house embedded in a local set of narratives. Over the last several
centuries the Western tradition has framed itself within a narrative assumption that tends to universalize its own self-understanding to the rest
of the world. The result of this perceived hegemony is that a moment in
history came to be taken as the primary reference point for the church in
all places and at all times. Its structures, therefore, ceased to be seen
primarily as finite and local, but universalized as normative.

It must be asked, for example, if the Eurocentric forms of the church
handed down from the Reformation are still viable. Why were they universalized as the forms of church for so many? The answer lies in the
unique moment in history when philosophy and technology melded
into a theology of empire, progress and the universalizing authority of
the Western narrative under God's sovereign plan for history. Why is it
that in our use of language the religious events of sixteenth-century
Europe continue to shape our interpretations of God's agency in the
world today?

There is much at stake here in terms of discernment and understanding
God's agency in our time. Are the ways this sixteenth-century Reformation and its radical reactions structured the church normatively for all
time and places? At the same time, structures of church life much older
than the sixteenth century are providing profound mediating meaning

across multiple generations. How do we discern what the Spirit is doing in the midst of all this dislocation? The answers are not simple!

SUMMARY

This chapter has framed the discussion of structure and institutional-ization within the church. Like practically every other institution in the Western world, church systems are in the midst of massive changes we still do not understand. We dwell in the midst of the whirlwind without the privilege of some high ground from which to observe all the forces contributing to the chaos. It is impossible to predict where this is going or propose alternative structures with certainty.

Structures and institutions are a concretization of the ways a society or community gives material form to its underlying narratives. They are the expressions of what a group believes to be its deepest convictions, values, perspectives and stories within a larger society. As such, struc-tures and institutions go deep into the imaginative life of a community. They are precritical in the sense that a people come to take them for granted because they have become an essential way in which a group expresses its identity and shapes its life. Structures and institutions lose their power to shape a people when these underlying narratives and stories cease to assist people in making sense of the world they live in. One suspects that the Spirit is in the process of tearing down some, or much, of existing denominational and church structure, but the critical piece is to engage in theological discernment (What is God up to?) and resist the move to too quickly changing structures. Chapter five provides examples of this reality in the twentieth century.

5

Legitimating Narratives

*Structures and the Churches
in the Twentieth Century*

INTRODUCTION

This chapter seeks to clear the window a little (using Pelikan's metaphor) in order to see some of the sources of the structures and institutions we have inherited from the twentieth century. It identifies some of the legitimating narratives that informed the structuring of the church in that period and offers reasons why elements of those narratives lost legitimacy by the end of the last millennium. It is limited to those churches formed out of Eurotribal immigrations and rooted in the sixteenth-century European reformations.

Structures are more than written constitutions or books of discipline that outline how a group makes decisions, the roles of various leaders, or how meetings are conducted. To a large extent they are in place before we entered the world, and they therefore structure our world for us. This is a point Alasdair McIntyre made so well in *After Virtue* when he described how we are all born onto a stage where a play is already being performed. That stage is already filled with props and scenery that frame and give meaning to our place and role on the stage and in the script. The structures of local, national and regional church life were the stage on which the wrestling with the great unraveling of the Eurotribal churches took place. We will explore some of the narratives that lie behind these structures in order to see why we have the structures we have and why they can't simply be discarded like old plumbing.

STRUCTURES AND NARRATIVES

Before moving to illustrations of this interrelationship between narrative and structure in church systems, it will be helpful to offer several brief illustrations from other areas of life.

Forms of social life. In the New Testament we observe a variety of images describing how these young churches structured their life. In Jerusalem, as discussed earlier, people met in the temple and one another's houses. Later, in Paul's varied epistles the images are those of household and, initially, synagogue. A high value is placed on the household as a social structure critical to the church's life in this formative period. How do we read what these texts mean by household or house?

If we look at the structures of our contemporary households as the template for reading these texts, it would be easy to misconceive what was going on in the early church. The primary paradigm in our culture has been what is known as the nuclear family. Since the last decades of the twentieth century, that structure of social life has attenuated to the point where a majority of adults in North America live as either one-parent households or alone. The structure of household in the New Testament period expressed a radically different narrative from our own time. By comparison, these were large extended families composed of generations, with relatives living together along with workers. They were usually extended economic communities formed around skills, trades, services, product development, farming or business. The source of this structuring was a way of understanding how the world ought to work and how a culture was to provide the good things in life for one another (a legitimating narrative). People's identities formed around this larger sense of being a household. In our time a radically different set of narratives has been at work in order to make sense of a fundamentally different structuring of household. The narratives about economic life and how to provide the good things in life for one another seem to be shaped by a narrative of personal expression and individualism. Household no longer means extended community but individual expression. While the word *household* is the same word for both contexts in English, the underlying legitimating narratives are profoundly different and produce radically different structural expressions.

The structure of buildings. One of the most interesting conflicts around legitimating narratives shaping human community in cities occurred around the midpoint of the twentieth century. The person who embodied this conflict of narratives was Jane Jacobs.[1] Only brief comments will be offered here about her work to illustrate differing narratives. During the early part of the twentieth century a certain kind of architecture dominated household and commercial construction. Known as "modernism," it featured extremely functional building design in high-rise buildings. Living was separated from work and commercial areas. The high-rise buildings were provided with large parking areas and, at the time, green areas for recreation. People drove home from work or shopping, went into their apartments, shut their doors and lived efficient, separate lives. These modernist structures expressed a narrative about how human beings might thrive. It codified in buildings and urban design a conviction that the best model for giving people the good things in life was the efficiency and rationality of early twentieth-century industrialization and its technological developments. Jacobs argued, persuasively, that this legitimating narrative and the structures of living it produced were in fact diminishing human life. She proposed low-rise (three to four stories), mixed-purpose (residential on the upper levels and commercial at the street level) buildings with wide sidewalks where people could intermingle and engage one another for the thriving of urban life. It is quite easy to see that these two radically different structures of urban life express two underlying but divergent narratives about how to thrive as human communities. These underlying narratives get lived out in concrete forms of structures.

A STOREHOUSE OF NARRATIVES AND THEIR SOCIAL STRUCTURES

The organizational and structural forms of church life in North America are also expressions of legitimating narratives. Critiques of the church based on dichotomies between institutional and organic structures fail to get at the question of informing narratives. It is quite normal for all of us to assume that the organizational structures we've been born in (nuclear family, corporation, union, voluntary society, certain forms of church) are just the way things are. This is why it's important to pause to understand the underlying sources of our structures and reflect on the narratives that form them.

As human beings we have a huge capacity to create meaning out of the storehouses of narratives, metaphors and myths that comprise our world. This rich, fertile soil of stories, narrative, memories and experiences passed down through generations come together, forming and reforming in a myriad of ways to make a culture.[2] We live together out of the deep, subterranean magma of all these stories and experiences. There is no logic or code that could unlock or lay bare how a culture is continually being formed and reformed out of all this rich, churning mixture.[3] This is what makes Christianity so profoundly important and rich. Over time the gospel has come to be embodied in a constellation of multiple cultures and narratives, none of which alone constitutes the whole of the gospel. Within cultures, narratives coalesce and form a social community that comes to life as a whole lot of people come to find in them a legitimating narrative for who they are and how they will live.

The capacity of a narrative (within a culture and at particular periods of time) to provide a framework people believe gives them a means of successfully ordering their life is what gives that narrative its legitimacy. Organizations, like governments, educational institutions, denominations or local churches, lose that legitimacy when their underlying narratives no longer provide that explanatory framework for growing numbers of people. Such a loss of legitimacy has been happening to the Protestant Eurotribal churches in North America. They confront a legitimacy crisis.[4] The challenge here isn't primarily changing structures but understanding the nature of this crisis.

Every culture forms varieties of social systems that structure the means by which people relate to one another in terms of roles, identity and meaning. These systems range from political institutions, schools, local churches, denominations, families, professional associations and so on. They are the structured concretization of a society's legitimating narratives. Over time this organization and role structuring solidifies into traditions, habits, ways of operating, means of joining, rules of belonging, hierarchies of power, books of discipline. They eventually become the taken-for-granted ways of defining how people function and relate to one another. For the members of a social system, such as a family, church, business organization, professional association and the like, such structured ways of life become implicit. Social and organizational structures, therefore, provide a powerful, symbolically integrated meaning system for members structuring their relationships with one another and the larger context. In this way a social system structures people within its traditions. This is why some are Mennonites, some Lutherans, others Presbyterians and so forth.

This reality was vividly illustrated for me several years ago while working with a group of Christian Reformed pastors. Some background to this denomination will help frame the context. In Canada the Christian Reformed Church's heritage is that of Dutch immigrants in early to mid-twentieth century. As these Dutch immigrants settled and established themselves in various parts of the country, second and third generations understood that their fundamental church heritage was also an ethnic heritage. Their ways of structuring life together came directly from the narratives of their Dutch heritage and traditions. One of the ways this was done was through educational systems (itself a definitive structure that forms a common life). They had established Christian elementary and high schools as well as a string of colleges and universities across North America (for example, Redeemer, Dordt and Calvin Colleges) to which most of their children went. This structuring of schools and colleges came out of a specific set of theological convictions about the nature of Christian formation in a society—in other words, a legitimating narrative. At some point in the last third of the twentieth century there was a move to broaden the base and scope of the church. As part of this move, the name of the denomination was changed from Dutch Reformed to Christian Reformed. This was not an insignificant attempt to create a narrative that would have legitimacy beyond that of Dutch immigrants and their children.

There were about seven pastors at the meeting. We met in one of their church buildings. Each pastor led a relatively large, successful congregation. The purpose of our meeting was to wrestle with the issues of being a missional church in their context. As we engaged with one another in discussion throughout the day, I felt at home with them. Around five in the afternoon we went out for dinner. Discussions continued with the same animation. By the time we returned to the church, it was dark but lights were on all through the building. You might imagine eight of us walking into the building from the parking lot. As we crossed the outside doors into the large foyer, where many people moved back and forth, those pastors all started speaking to the people there in Dutch. I suddenly became a complete outsider. In that moment it was clear how deep our narratives go and how powerfully they shape our default actions. None of those pastors had any intention of leaving me out, but they had just entered a cultural world where their narratives were structured in the very language they used with one another. The narratives inside us structure us into social systems that function as powerfully shaping defaults.

LEGITIMATING NARRATIVES AND THE ROLE OF STRUCTURE

Organizational structures embody and guarantee the continuity of a group's tradition. They codify, systematize and embody the implicit values and commitments of a group. Such structures come to be identified as the culture of a people. This is what was happening when I returned to the church building with these Christian Reformed ministers that evening.

These organizational structures require people to function inside a set of roles that eventually become taken for granted and seem to be just the way things are supposed to be done. Such roles predefine how people function and relate to each other. Leaders are trained in and carry out (perform) expected roles developed within the organization over a long period of time. What we fail to notice is how these roles actually change as the legitimating narratives of a culture change, while the words used to describe them don't. This is why traditions are complex. We have to be attentive to how changing cultural narratives shift the assumptions a group has about the nature of its organization and the roles people have within it. We tend to keep using the same language around structures and roles, but lose sight of how their actual functionality is being changed by changing cultural narratives.

The role of pastor is an illustration. The role is continually being re-

shaped by cultural narratives most people don't reflect on. The consequences are significant. The word *pastor* (teaching elder, priest, etc.) has
remained fairly stable in usage for several centuries. The role expectations that lie inside that word, however, keep changing. Several examples
of this will suffice.

Prior to the midpoint of the twentieth century one would have been
hard pressed to understand the role of pastor in clinical or therapeutic
terms. That is certainly not the case today. Beginning in the early 1960s it
is possible to detect a shift in the meaning of the pastoral role. It began as
a small trickle and by the end of that century had become an avalanche
that radically changed the role of pastor. Yet the word *pastor* didn't change.
This happened with little protest or awareness of what was occurring because the legitimating narratives of the wider culture were going through
massive upheavals and transformations. From the 1960s forward the
notion of pastor as counselor (the therapeutic approaches of the human
potential movement focused on the self-actualization and development of
the autonomous self) became the dominant metaphor for pastoral care.
Seminaries that developed a specialized master of divinity degree in counseling were quickly oversubscribed (while those in theology or biblical
studies could hardly get enough students to justify a class). Clinical Pastoral Education was made a requirement in a majority of schools and ordination processes. The more classic role of pastor as spiritual guide focused on the formation of disciples almost disappeared. Behind this identity
change lay deeper changes in legitimating narratives. Stated briefly, just as
the focus of the wider society became that of the self-actualizing individual
(counselors and therapists were the new priests),[5] so the pastoral role
shifted from forming people in practices shaped by God as the focal center
of life to that of a god who helped people self-develop. We still see this
today in the levels of counseling and therapy pastors offer as well as in the
language of meeting people's "needs" and becoming "seeker sensitive."

A second illustration of how the word *pastor* was maintained while the
role shifted also developed in the last quarter of the twentieth century.
This was the model of the pastor as manager of a local franchise of the
corporate denomination. Pastors were trained in seminary through a
common curriculum model developed and agreed to through their mem-

bership in Association of Theological Schools. The model was, basically, the idea of pastor as manager. The legitimating narrative said: If one manages well the systems, processes and programs handed down from the experts and professionals in the corporate denominations and their training schools, then the good things in life will be ours. For some fifty years or more this legitimating narrative, and its organizational structures, was successful.

CONCRETIZING LEGITIMATING NARRATIVES

Groups create organizational structures that concretize and instantiate their deepest narratives. These structures determine the roles in which people are expected to perform, with excellence, those activities deemed important and appropriate for the system's maintenance, thriving and survival. There is little that is permanent, however, in these roles. As pointed out earlier, even when the language remains the same, the meaning keeps changing as the deeper legitimating narratives of the culture change.

Organizational structures habituate people into a way of life (Baptists, Presbyterians and Anglicans behave differently, with differing expectations for their church life). They provide people with the pathways for taking on and monitoring the language games, habits, attitudes and values of the group. They provide the rationale for the roles and expectations of people within the group. Such structures concretize a group's underlying narratives. Organizational structures do this in a variety of interconnected ways:

- Locating people in roles, contexts and relationships that interpret the overarching narratives

- Structuring roles and rules that channel the system's direction, purpose and future

- Becoming mechanisms for living out the purpose of the social system. In a local church, for example, these would be seen in such things as liturgies, catechesis, small groups, architecture of the worship space, terminology for the worship space (*sanctuary* and *meeting house* are not the same narratives) and so forth

- Providing a means by which a group can cultivate its values, develop transferable habits and sustain continuity of the system over time

- Providing a matrix for recognizing the boundaries in which the system can function and maintain identity

A group's culture develops over time through several critical interactions between its store of core narratives and the legitimating narratives of the environment it lives in. This culture, with its passed-on stories, habits, attitudes and practices, is continually being formed and re-formed through processes of testing, experimenting, norming, organizing and structuring that provide people with rich levels of roles and functions. Over time these elements, in complex interactions with each other and the environment, give a group or society a structural identity that provides a meaning system for its people. In these interactions the people in a social group give loyalty to organizational structures to the extent that these structures empower them to make sense of their world within a larger, cultural system. When structures cease to serve this purpose, however, they lose their power to hold, inform and give meaning to people. It means the structural systems are increasingly making less and less sense of cultural narratives for the members of the group. When this occurs, organizational structures that once mediated and inculturated a group's narratives lose their legitimacy. This is happening to denominational systems and the organizational structures in Western societies.

LEGITIMACY

Legitimacy concerns the way people commit and give their loyalty to a social group and its organizational structures. The social theorist Jürgen Habermas uses the language of "legitimation" to express the sense people in a community or nation have when the institutional structures they live within are working in just, helpful, benevolent ways that serve their sense of what is right, and, therefore, deserve their support, loyalty and adherence.[6] When a majority of people in a social group experience organizational structures in this way, these structures and their underlying narratives have high legitimacy. Legitimacy, then, is clearly linked to social order within a group, organization or nation. Currently, for example, the so-called Arab Spring that swept across numbers of nations indicates that the social and organizational systems framed by generations of dictators have lost their legitimacy for a rising percentage of people. The massive shifts that moved across Egypt in the early part of 2011, overturning the forty-year, structurally embedded dictatorship of Hosni Mubarak offer a stark illustration of what happens when a legitimating narrative ceases to match the aspirations and underlying narratives of a people.

For reasons that are often difficult to explain, a culture shifts. In the molten centers that form and reshape societies, ordinary people become less and less confident in the narratives and structures they find themselves in. They sense that these narratives and structures somehow don't match with other narratives at work within them. When this happens existing narratives come under question, and the structures that gave them legitimation are rejected. This concept of legitimation explains why many Protestant denominations thrived until the mid-1970s. From that point on, underlying forces, gestating in the magma of Western societies, broke into public discourse to challenge and undermine once dominant public legitimating narratives. When this eruption of disaffection and resistance breaks open into public discourse in the larger culture, existing organizational structures can quickly lose their legitimacy.

This is not a new thing; it is just that North American society experienced an exceptionally long period in which specific legitimating narratives were so dominant that they came to be assumed as unchallengeable norms. But history is replete with moments when the structural and legitimating narratives of a society or group come to an end. The European Reformation of the sixteenth century, for example, broke up the overarching legitimating narrative of the Roman Catholic Church at the time. In eighteenth-century France, the ancien régime was violently overthrown by the French Revolution as a precursor for massive social revolutions all over Europe. The cultural upheavals in the 1960s and 1970s signaled a period when existing legitimating narratives and the structural systems that gave them life were overturned. Throughout Europe and North America it was a period when organizational structures ceased to hold people's loyalty. In summary, when over an extended period of time sufficient numbers of people place their trust, confidence, loyalty and belief in the social system because of the identity it provides, the organizational culture it creates will have high levels of legitimacy. But when sufficient numbers lose confidence in the capacity of those structures to carry the narratives they live in, legitimacy is lost.

What is it that at one time causes people to give high levels of legitimation to a social system's organizational structures and then quite quickly lose that legitimation? A social system (nation, corporation, family, local church or denomination) is not an abstraction. It is a living organism operating within a complex cultural environment comprising all the implicit and explicit narratives and stories of all the systems interacting with it. A social system thrives as it innovates successful adaptations with this complex environment. When the cultural environment is stable and coherent over a significant period of time, a social system develops a homeostatic relationship through the effective use of learned, performative skills. The system adapts to the point where its structures and systems match and work well within the larger cultural environment.

An example of this was the way many Protestant denominations adopted the organizational structure of the twentieth-century corporation. From the 1920s to the mid-1970s this corporate denomination organizational structure worked brilliantly because it matched the larger legitimating narrative of American corporate culture. A narrative of rationalized efficiency, professional management, bureaucratic structures, hierarchy and high program management shaped it. The congruence between the dominant narratives of the wider culture and the organizational life of the denominations contributed to the high levels of social legitimacy given to these churches. But larger cultural environments don't remain static or stable forever. At some point cultures change. This happened, for example, in the radical societal shifts starting in the 1960s, along with fundamental changes in organizational cultures from the late 1970s onward through the globalization of trade starting in the mid-1980s. These were seismic changes in the underlying social, political, communicative and religious narratives.[7] When such change happens in the narratives of a social system, its legitimating structures are called into question. When this occurs, the performative skills developed to carry forward those structures are insufficient for the system's life, and adaptive skills must be quickly identified or the system dies.

DENOMINATIONS AND TWENTIETH-CENTURY LEGITIMATING NARRATIVES

This dynamic is now at play across the Eurotribal Protestant denominations of North America. For much of the twentieth century they formed themselves around the legitimating narrative of the corporation. The malaise of denominations is that they continue to struggle with how to reimagine this narrative when it is no longer sustainable. This is a story mirrored in most Protestant churches and provides insight into what has been occurring in church systems over the last several decades.

The emergence of the corporate organization at the end of the nineteenth century was an adaptive response to rapid industrialization, technological innovation and economic development in the second half of the nineteenth century. In the early twentieth century, denominations consciously took on the organizational forms of this corporate culture, reflecting this massive shift in legitimacy across North American culture. The legitimacy of denominational systems throughout the twentieth century, therefore, lay not in their theological distinctives, nor in some understanding of the gospel, but in their capacity to mirror the corporation in its delivery of the goods and services (religious in this case) of any major, brand name corporation (local churches became franchises or branch offices). This adaptation enabled churches to flourish in a growing market economy, but it proved fatal in terms of an identity shaped by the traditions out of which these denominations were formed.

The corporate denomination's organizational structures mirrored the practices of their larger context. Leadership functions emerged that enabled these churches to supply branded religious goods and services. To the extent that the larger corporatist environment remained stable, undergoing primarily continuous, developmental change, the legitimacy of the churches in the larger culture was high. This was the case because the internal mechanisms (organizational rules of operation and performance) of the denominations effectively maintained a dynamic balance with the larger environment. They developed maximum organizational functionality within the corporatist model. In this context leaders (at national, regional and local levels of the church) took on as their primary skill sets the roles of managers, experts and professionals that any corporatist organization requires to effectively deliver its brand-name goods and services. In this way the denominations thrived because what they offered, religiously, correlated with and made sense of the lives and functions of church members who lived and worked in the larger corporatist culture. The attitudes and beliefs; the knowledge base; the skills and the transferable habits of the denominations had high levels of congruence with the larger environment. In this setting the churches enjoyed high levels of legitimacy because they created structural stability within that environment and therefore functioned as a powerful source of social integration and patterning. In this sense organizational cultures of the churches offered people another social system of stability, continuity, consistency and meaning within the larger corporatist culture.

But change happens whether we're prepared or not! When significant levels of change occur in the larger environment that are neither understood nor matched by corresponding responses from within social systems such as denominations (national-regional-local systems), a crisis of legitimacy occurs. Identity is called into question by its constituency and the wider culture. Its leaders are confronted by questions about their assumed competencies and roles. Habermas points out, "Crisis in social systems is not produced through accidental changes in the environment but through structurally inherent system-imperatives that are incompatible and cannot be hierarchically integrated."[8] In other words, the problem is not in the environment, with all its massive change, but the internal structural systems of the denominations with their deeply embedded implicit assumptions about how the organization ought to function, what roles people ought to have, and what the goods and ends are of the organization. This inability of the system to internally grasp what is at stake creates the crisis of legitimation. But the crisis is not primarily about structures; it is about the internalized, taken-for-granted narratives.

It is difficult to recognize that the very attitudes and beliefs, knowledge bases, skills and habits that were shaped interactively with the environment over a long period of time need to be addressed. Rather, turning from these fundamental expressions of social imaginaries, leaders focus on adjusting and fixing structures. The more this takes place (and this is what is going on across most denominational systems), the churches and their leaders cease to have the capacity to provide the explanatory frameworks for people within an environment of rapid, discontinuous change. At this point both the social system's organizational forms and the tradition on which they have been formed are called into question by growing numbers of its members; its interpretive systems "lose their social integrative power," which "serves as an indicator of the collapse of the social system."[9]

This is an argument about the level or kind of challenge confronting denominations. They are confronted with a legitimation crisis of significant proportions. This level of challenge cannot be addressed with tactical or programmatic strategies. The more a denomination builds its response on programmatic tactics and strategies of organizational change, the deeper and faster the loss of legitimacy.

Figure 5.1 presents three levels at which an organizational system functions: (A) culture, (B) organizational system, and (C) leadership or role functionality. In discontinuous environmental change the legitimating narratives that have shaped a culture over some period of time are being called into question. People are losing their confidence in these narratives. Because such narratives are implicit (usually assumed and taken for granted), most people do not recognize that this is the source of their sense of dis-ease and loss of confidence. It is this level, however, that must be addressed in a change process. Rather than recognizing this as the critical place of engagement, denominational systems turn their energies to the other two levels of system function. They turn their attention toward the levels of organizational structure and role identity (because this is where their expertise, experience and skills are located, and hence their comfort level in management and control of anxiety). But these levels are a product and function of the first, the level of cultural narratives. Changing structures and roles does not address the question of culture. Figure 5.1 illustrates these three levels. The core of a social system is the culture it creates. Organizational and role functions are expressions of how the cultural narratives get lived out in an environment.

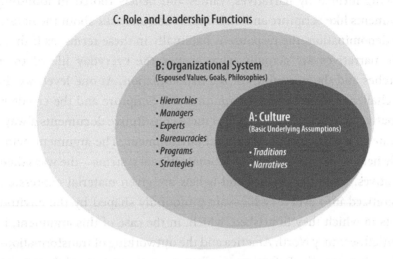

C: Role and Leadership Functions

B: Organizational System
(Espoused Values, Goals, Philosophies)

• *Hierarchies*
• *Managers*
• *Experts*
• *Bureaucracies*
• *Programs*
• *Strategies*

A: Culture
(Basic Underlying Assumptions)

• *Traditions*
• *Narratives*

Figure 5.1. Denomination as social system

Currently the energy in denominational systems is directed at levels B and C where they seek to address such elements as

• reorganization of structure

• reframing of policy and procedure manuals

• development of programs and strategies that address areas such as church revitalization, growth, evangelism and new church development

• leadership training programs

• role redefinitions (e.g., from pastor to apostle, etc.)

• personnel reductions in the light of falling budgets

Each represents a tactical response that fails to address the cultural transformations underlying the experiences of change, discontent and loss.[10]

In liminal situations, reordering structures, introducing programs and redefining leadership will not address the legitimation issues.[11] The underlying basis of the actual narratives, traditions, values and beliefs of the churches needs to be addressed. This requires some explanation and qualification.

Congregations and denominational systems tend to view themselves as being formed by narratives, values and beliefs rooted in founding documents like Scripture and tradition. When one asks about the nature of a denomination, the response is habitually in these terms, as if these basic narratives are actually what shapes the everyday life of their churches and the operations of the denomination. At one level, we do not challenge these claims. Commitment to Scripture and the creeds is formative for Christian identity. But these constitutive documents always operate in a particular sociocultural environment. The argument being made here is that the cultures of denominational systems—the ways their narratives, traditions, values and beliefs are given material expression, concretized into everyday life—are profoundly shaped by the environments in which they flourished, which, in the case of this argument, is twentieth-century North America and the outworking of transformations in the West since the Reformation. Chapter six maps some of these transformations in legitimating narratives.

Changing Legitimacy—
Changing Frameworks

THE FUNCTION OF ORGANIZATIONAL SYSTEMS

Organizational systems embody the meaning systems of their members (a shared pattern of basic assumptions that the group has learned as it solved its problems of external adaptation and internal integration). They serve a variety of critical roles in culture as a means of addressing specific needs within a cultural context. They establish the mechanisms, roles and structures by which a group makes meaning and functions in its environment.

Through much of the twentieth century, Protestant America did this through the corporate denomination. Its mechanisms and structures had a high correlation with the forms of organizational life its members experienced daily in business, commerce, education and politics. It was an organizational form that functionally embodied the narrative imagination of the period. The challenge is that in the midst of overarching culture change, particular organizational systems with their rules, norms, policies, procedures, management and leadership practices can cease to provide the means whereby members can meaningfully engage a changing social environment. While it is absolutely necessary to then look for ways to change the institutional and organizational systems, the proposal of this book is to do this through an engagement with the underlying narratives that have been shaping these systems in order to discern what is actually at work.

In the latter part of the twentieth century the larger cultural environments of modernity, industrial capitalism and the state underwent massive transformations resulting in the delegitimization of the very forms of social life developed in the early part of the century. Denominations lost their legitimacy and are now characterized by growing levels of internal and external contradictions. It is time to reflect more deeply on these cultural transformations.

TWO THIRTY-YEARS WARS AND CULTURAL TRANSFORMATIONS

Stephen Toulmin, who was a philosopher at the University of Chicago, proposed that the political, religious and intellectual frameworks that formed the West over some three hundred years can be understood around two principal events: (1) the first Thirty Years' War, which resulted in the Peace of Westphalia in 1648, and (2) the second Thirty Years' War, from 1914–1945, which resulted in the end of the age of modernity.[1] Westphalia legitimated the formation of a coherent, interconnected political, religious and intellectual imagination; by the end of World War II these same societies were again being transformed around changing forms of political, religious and intellectual life.[2] The following summarizes the characteristic forms of legitimacy that emerged after Westphalia in 1648.

Political formation. Westphalia established sovereign states ruled by princes or kings as the legitimate form of government in Europe. By treaty these states had agreed on borders intended to secure a stable, predictable and manageable Europe. They consented not to interfere in each other's internal life. This fostered the emergence of a new kind of political system, the modern state.[3]

Religious formation. Europe in the seventeenth century was a Christian society. Churches remained at the center of social and cultural influence. This would gradually erode as the state, secularization and economic transformation shifted the churches into the private sector of personal morality in an emerging bipolar world.[4] Under the influence of Immanuel Kant, ethics shifted toward personal morality internalized in the individual self, resulting in an effectively privatized church.[5]

As a means of ending the destructive religious wars that followed the

Reformation, Westphalia established the principle of *cuius regio, eius religio* (the religion of the ruler is the religion of the region), leading to the establishment of official state churches. Alternative religious choice within the states was either marginally tolerated (for political reasons) or persecuted because it was viewed as disloyal. Post-Westphalian Europe had little patience for religious groups that challenged the new clarity, certainty and ordered world that had been created.

Intellectual formation. The sixteenth and seventeenth centuries' anxious search for certainty produced a new view of reason that led to a revolution in the nature of understanding and truth. Enlightenment thinkers sought a new foundation for knowing on which to build a manageable, human-centered civilization. This foundation was built on the conviction that a new axial point for certainty had been discovered in the self. Human reason, from within itself alone, could uncover the nature of truth through a process based on abstract, universal laws apprehensible by human reason alone. Such an understanding of truth was welcomed as a profound breakthrough that would guarantee a world of predictability, certainty and eventually, human control over the forces of nature. The intellectual transformations of the period, built on Cartesian abstract rationality (the foundational point of certainty outside the ephemeral, changing, material world), Baconian empiricism, Kantian reason and Newtonian physics provided the foundations upon which the modern world was built.

One of the results of all this creative rethinking and reimagining of the basis of knowledge was a gradual sense that the ordinary and everyday could not be trusted, but that the resources of the mind could be the true basis for knowledge.[6] The local, everyday and the ordinary were viewed as unreliable sources of knowing grounded in ignorance and emotions. As a result, trust diminished in the local and everyday as sources of knowledge, stability, predictability and security. The local and particular represented a form of understanding that had led to all the terrible strife and awful uncertainty of the previous period. The clearest example of this irrationality of the local and ordinary was religious belief. Its roots were seen as lying in experience and feelings. In the outbreak of the terrible wars of the early seventeenth century, each religious group had claimed it had *the* truth, killing those of other groups who would not align themselves with that truth. The new understanding of reason removed this dependence on the local and removed experience from the equation as it gave priority to fact over faith, reason over belief.

In the seventeenth and eighteenth centuries the notion of rationality as universal and abstract became the dominant narrative in the development of the political order of the emerging states. As Toulmin points out, the idea of *rational government*, so common to the modern mind, constituted a wholly new conception and practice. Politics and government now came to be understood as forces capable of shaping the social and organizational frameworks of all human life. The idea that society was "manmade" emerged; the notion that the state could actually make society through the appropriated application of scientific and technical rationality came to dominate the imagination of the modern world. At the same time, in post–Westphalian Europe, an unheard of mobilization of resources and people through the state indicated that the human making of society was not a utopian dream but a viable possibility.[7]

Similarly, the *rational individual* became the dominant understanding of the human ideal. For sociologist Zygmunt Bauman, this was a novel and revolutionary way of understanding human life. A wholly new concept of the human emerged, whose actions are shaped entirely by his or her own self-knowledge. Modernity wagered that it could make, form, and control the world through the internal, rational and moral life of individuals without any reference to a transcendent authority.[8] The rational individual of modernity is the self-making, moral individual of Kant's bold Enlightenment manifesto.[9] Bauman argues that a new vision of the individual emerged in which the self was constantly malleable in its ability to redirect thought and behavior through rational knowledge and expert technique.

All this was to be made possible through the offices of the newly emerging experts. These were the new high priests of modern culture. They were people who, as the possessors of true knowledge, could create the circumstances of a better, predictable and certain world through the rational application of their skills. These were the people "in the know" who, through the new hierarchies of government, educational institutions and other systems developed through the new social sciences, could create a new kind of social order and a new form of individual life.

When these political, social, religious and intellectual movements were being born in the late sixteenth and early seventeenth centuries, they did not have to fight their way forward. An old world lay exhausted before people in so many ways by 1648. The legitimacies of the medieval world with its political, religious and intellectual formations had been called deeply into question. This revolutionary period brought into existence new forms of political, religious and intellectual life looking for a new form of social organization that would both integrate society and provide a much needed new form of legitimation.

Together these three elements—political, religious and intellectual— forged a new legitimation narrative with a distinct organizational culture displaying a common set of characteristics summarized as follows:

- They were *bounded-set systems*. State, religion and universal rationality tolerated no alternative forms. There could be no other forms but the nation-state states; there would be only one religion in each state, and the categories of Enlightenment rationality were the determinative forms of reasoning. This bounded-set system came to be known as the secular state.

- Each operated from *top-down organizational functionalities*. The state ruled from king down; the church had its own hierarchy that determined the nature of religious life for all; and the intellectual environment placed universal, mathematized, abstract rationality as the highest form of reasoning. All other forms fell beneath in a hierarchy of value in which local experience was farthest removed from truth.

- It functioned within a *performative world* of predictability, manageability, control and linearity. This should come as little surprise since the underlying impetus shaping this social imaginary was the search for predictability and certainty. The underlying dynamic driving the formation of modernity's legitimacy was the need to form a world characterized by nonambiguity, predictability, control and efficiency.

Cultural systems create organizational systems designed to put into action the forms of legitimation created in their basic narratives, founding myths and traditions. Through the eighteenth and nineteenth centuries a series of forces developed around this legitimizing myth which, by the late nineteenth century, contributed to the emergence of the modern corporation.[10] This understanding of the corporation entered and profoundly shaped the nature of religious life in North America throughout most of the twentieth century.

THE CORPORATE ORGANIZATIONAL CULTURE

Out of this new legitimation narrative developed specific organizational forms from the late nineteenth through to the late twentieth centuries that, for almost a century, became the normative organizational culture undergirding Western societies shaped by an abstractionist, universalizing, functional rationality. By the last quarter of the twentieth century the formative legitimating narratives coming out of Westphalia were going through massive renegotiation. That process is summarized in the political, religious and intellectual spheres:

Political. The nation-state transformed into another entity identified by Manuel Castells, Philip Bobbitt and others as the *market state.* Some declare the end of the nation-state with the emergence of globalized political and economic institutions; others see the reemergence of old divides involving the clash of civilizations, while others predict the reemergence of older nationalisms reinforcing subterranean tribal identities. All of which is to say that by the beginning of the twenty-first century the political situation is in great flux, with little clarity on what might emerge.[11] Some level of consensus exists in the recognition that in the West the state is transforming into the market state in the midst of something called globalization.

Religious. The notion of any form of established church disappears. In America, where the denominations took the place of an established church very early in its history, what did exist for much of this time was the experience of a cultural domain enjoyed by many of the denominations. Their organizational systems assumed this domain. This is now over. Its ending creates anxiety and confusion across the churches. A social legitimacy has disappeared. The churches find themselves competing in a globalized and pluralist religious market where people shop for their own unique forms of spirituality. Denominations, and their churches, find themselves in a liminal situation seeking to understand how their organizational systems function in this new context.

Intellectual. The certitude of an abstract, universal rationality that supplied the key to reason and truth has been demolished. A situation is emerging in which reason is again coming to be understood from within the perspective of local, temporal and sensual realities of everyday life. A radically different perspective on the source and nature of truth is solidifying in the West in which the narratives of local, particular peoples and contexts become the rich texture for the formation of understanding. What is emerging is a new kind of intermixing where the expert and professional are forming co-learning environments with a renewing sense of the wisdom and importance of the local and particular. Networks of people with various skills and capacities are being seen again as critical elements in addressing the new contexts of change.[12] Everyday experience within the practical lives of ordinary people receives greater valence than that of the previously constructed world of experts and professionals.[13] Networks of learning take on greater importance than hierarchies of authority. The importance of narrative and story displaces that of abstract ideas and principles. The implicit value of varieties of models and frameworks replaces that of a monadic system generalized for everyone in all places.

These enormous shifts bring about consequent transformations in organizational cultures and the relationship of the individual to them. By the end of the twentieth century new forms of social and organizational culture were emerging that are affecting and undermining the legitimacy and function of denominational systems. Such changes need to be explored to understand their implications for the churches and denominational systems.

TRANSFORMING SOCIAL LANDSCAPE AT THE START OF THE THIRD MILLENNIUM

Manuel Castells argues that by the end of the second millennium of the Christian era a series of changes of historical significance transformed the social landscape of the world. While global in character, these changes emerged primarily in the West. Their effects on organizational cultures are profound. Churches and denominations, as organizational cultures, are not exempt from this analysis. Denominational systems are implicated in changes now forging a new culture in the West. Castells identifies these changes as follows:

1. *Technological revolution.* Technological revolution involves the rapid development, introduction and diffusion of information technologies to all levels of social interaction.

2. *Transformed economies.* Ending the Cold War meant a rapid end of national economies and the emergence of an unequal, interdependent globalized economy forging new relationships between economy, state and society.

3. *Capitalism and globalization.* From the late 1980s forward capitalism undergoes restructuring. It is disembedded from primary attachments to national economies, moving unimpeded to any part of the world.

4. *Role of the state.* In the West the state, not a helpless bystander, is a primary player in the transformation of capitalism through:

   • *Deregulation.* Legislation to deregulate markets and create open borders for business organizations. Information technology makes it increasingly impossible to police or manage the flow of capital. Western nations removed tariff barriers to increase the ability of business organizations within their own borders to expand markets around the world.

   • *Privatization.* Once publicly owned systems are privatized to reduce government costs and create an environment to attract capital.

   • *Erosion of social safety nets.* To compete in global markets Western nations quickly undid safety nets to reduce levels of cost and taxation, shifting the social burden onto citizens.

5. *Decentralization.* Production and manufacturing are decentralized around the globe.

6. *Networking.* The primary form of information exchange comes through networking.

7. *Changing forms of individualization.* There are two sides to changing

forms of individualization.[14] First, some argue modernity has built-in contradictions that undermine its functionalities. Thus, the forces of capitalism disembed people from primary relationships.[15] The result is that people feel cast upon themselves, sensing that the social contract between state and people, shaped in the nineteenth and twentieth centuries, has been torn up. People thus feel in the grip of unnamed, unseen forces determining their lives and over which they have no control. Second, Ulrich Beck and Anthony Giddens argue the driving force of change is not the structural and functional forms of life in modernity as much as individuation itself. What happened in the later part of the twentieth century is that the individuation process breaks free from the structures of modernity as people are more and more able to reflect on the nature of their relationship with these structures. Individuals become agents who self-define their relationship to social structures. These are two interpretations of the same phenomenon—a rapid individuation of society where individuals no longer feel bound to social and organizational systems.[16]

8. *Obsolescence.* Skills and expertise developed over many years that guaranteed lifelong careers in the established organizational culture become obsolete due to technological innovation or outsourcing in a globalized market.

9. *Commodification.* An economized society transforms social relationships into commodities. People feel cut off from traditions that provided identity and sustained their lives.

10. *Turning inward.* As people are overwhelmed by the complexities and the inability of established social systems to provide coherent explanations, they turn inward.[17]

11. *Crises of legitimacy.* Political systems are engulfed in crises of legitimacy as people lose confidence in their capacity to address the critical challenges facing the world.

12. *Fragmented.* Social movements become fragmented, single-issue and ephemeral, unable to bind people together in a common narrative.

13. *Identity.* People cease to organize meaning around what they do and

who they are. In an uncontrolled, confusing world they regroup around religious, ethnic, territorial or national identities. But this regrouping is not like previous commitments and loyalties to religion, nation, group or land. It is shaped by retreat into identity groups, not solidarity in a larger narrative.

14. *Global networks of instrumental exchanges.* Global networks of instrumental exchanges emerge; they are celebrated as the new form of social interaction but are also perceived as systems that selectively switch individuals, groups, regions, and even countries on and off according to their functionality in fulfilling goals processed in the network of relentless economic decisions. If a group does not fit the strategic design for the increase of markets and flow of capital they are switched off as players in the global game.

15. *Alienation.* Alienation is a term coined by the Frankfurt School early in the twentieth century. It describes the inexorable effects of late capitalism in its commodification of people. For Castells it has a much broader meaning. People experience their lives as alienated from each other and see the other as a threat.

At the end of the twentieth century these transformations converged, creating a radical shift in social culture. By "the end of the twentieth century, we lived through one of these rare intervals in history" when human culture moved through a period of massive disruption and destabilization in which social organizations were transformed.[18] Giddens writes, "In the social sciences today, as in the social world itself, we face a new agenda. We live, as everyone knows, at a time of endings. . . . We are in a period of evident transition—and the 'we' here refers not only to the West but to the world as a whole."[19] These transformations affect denominations' very identity, not just their organizational structures.

THE LIMINAL SPACE OF THE CHURCHES

What do such massive changes mean for denominational systems formed in the early part of the twentieth century? What is the nature of the challenges confronting the innovation of missional life? When accepted forms of social legitimacy disappear, new ones slowly emerge and solidify.[20] But there is an in-between period of liminality in which people become aware that the ordered, performative world of the previous period is no longer operating but there is no clarity on what might emerge to take its place. We live in one of those times without clarity about the emerging alternatives.[21]

The crisis of the denominations is that few of their leaders understand the nature of the liminal situation or the scope of the transformations required. They continue looking for solutions that will repair current organizational forms without understanding that their legitimacy has melted away. This situation is critical. Denominations and congregations are perduring elements of the North American landscape. They are not going away, but they are being transformed. The logic of denominational and congregational life previously outlined and formed out of the twentieth century cannot serve us adequately as travelers in this liminal space. A different kind of imagination is required. Part two frames a series of proposals for engaging this new space.

PART TWO

REFRAMING OUR IMAGINATION

*The world is changed. I feel it in the water; I feel it in the earth;
I smell it in the air. Much that once was is lost and
none now liveth that remember it.*

Galadriel, in *Lord of the Rings*

Metaphors and Imagination

INTRODUCTION

Part two identifies key inhibiters that continue to shape the imagination (legitimating narratives) of the churches and proposes ways of framing the task at hand in the reimagination of church life. It does this within a self-conscious attempt to provide a missional hermeneutic for a renewed engagement of church structures with the emerging culture.

Answers to the challenges confronting the organizational systems of the Eurotribal churches outlined in part one seem more elusive than ever. Business as usual or working harder to improve existing structures and programs does not address the underlying issues. These denominations and their churches are in an in-between, liminal space. The skills and processes required to navigate this space remain elusive. Background metaphors continue to predetermine responses, preventing a reimagination of church life. These metaphors come from the formation of organizational life in the twentieth century. These underlying metaphors must be faced before a new imagination can emerge.

EXISTING FRAMEWORKS CAN'T ADDRESS THE CHALLENGES

The case can be stated simply: *Churches, at national, regional and local levels, face challenges that can't be addressed within existing frameworks.* The reality of a loss of confidence in national, regional and local church institutions must be addressed.[1] People are questioning the role of church organizational systems at every level. A world of instant communication, a plethora of choices and religious options are producing situations in which established self-understandings of the churches are under massive stress. In a multiracial, multicultural society, the challenges for long-established, monocultural churches of the European tradition described in part one are steep. What is at stake is not adjustment but something more demanding: a new imagination or what Ronald Heifetz describes as adaptive change. What will this involve?

GOD AS ACTIVE AGENT—BIBLICAL IMAGINATION—DISRUPTIVE FRAMEWORKS

How should those denominations that are the inheritors of Eurotribal immigrations and the Reformation stories interpret what is happening? What lenses should they use? Christian imagination, at its best, has sought to stand and see its context from a particular place that is in the name of the God revealed in Jesus Christ. Imaginative transformation is located in the place where we seek to discern what the Spirit might be up to in our time. Biblical texts are replete with narratives that continually push us back to this fundamental place. The place from which these churches have been asking what to do are the legitimating narratives outlined in part one. How might we adaptively learn to stand in a place where we perceive our situation in the name of God? The Bible gives us examples of how people are disoriented in order to see what God is doing with fresh eyes.

Exodus 2:23–3:12 tells parallel stories of the children of Israel groaning under bondage, Moses wandering in the backside of the wilderness with his father-in-law's flocks and the remembering of God. The stories of Israel and Moses at first appear as the primary focus of these narratives. They encapsulate the hard place Israel had come to, as well as the empty, in-between space this half Egyptian/half Hebrew finds himself. In differing ways each groaned; each was in a liminal space where their abilities to manage, control or predict outcomes were insufficient for the realities facing them when, after the course of those many days, the king of Egypt died. But the text is not telling a story primarily about either Israel or Moses; it is a story about God!

The writer of these texts labors to frame what's at stake for both in a context. It is about the capacity of each to grasp that their situations can only be understood and addressed by reframing their imaginations around the activities of God. There is an amazing juxtaposition of narrative in Exodus 3, where Moses witnesses the bush that burns but isn't consumed and declares: "I must turn aside and look at this great sight, and see why the bush is not burned up" (v. 3). The emphasis is on what we would term human agency, the central focus of our time, wherein Moses determines what he will do and how he will manage the situation. But the author will have none of this.

In the ensuing passages the narration between God and Moses reflects a basic shift in the use of the personal pronoun as if to indicate that Moses (and by implication Israel) cannot and will not be the primary agent in managing and controlling the outcomes of these liminal spaces (whether the groaning under bondage, wandering in the "beyond" of the desert or the bush that burns but is not consumed). The agent of this entire passage is God. Here, God is the agent of their past. (Note the rooting of God's agency in the story of Israel and the almost overuse of the pronoun *I* in juxtaposition to Moses' "I will turn aside.") What is so powerful about this passage is the way its narrator reengages the (lost) memory of Israel and Moses: God is reminding them who has been and therefore is still the agent of their lives.

In the midst of this establishment of agency over Moses' determinations and Israel's desire for changed outcomes stands Moses' own need to negotiate and manage the ways God will purposively deliver Israel. The story is well known: at each step of the negotiations God gives Moses a way forward but no control. (This comes later in the text with the giving of Aaron and the rod as well as Moses' request for God's name as the final means of acquiring control of outcomes.) In this passage Moses finally asks: "Who am I that I should go to Pharaoh, and bring the Israelites out of Egypt?"(Ex 3:11). Later, in response to the naming request, God's answer is: "I AM WHO I AM" (Ex 3:14)—an enigmatic response which minimally means: "It's none of your business, Moses. You can't have my name and you can't go with that kind of control!" In the present passage God's response to Moses' question, "Who am I?" is, "I will be with you; and this shall be the sign for you that it is I who sent you: when you have brought the people out of Egypt, you shall worship God on this

mountain" (Ex 3:12). The answer Moses gets, basically, is that he won't
know until he gets to the mountain with the people! This is a massive,
disruptive move into a new imagination that is no longer about management and control, but the agency of God in the midst of liminal space.
This is the imagination the churches have lost in our time.

CHANGING PERSPECTIVE

Within the disruptions affecting all sectors of society, the churches must
learn again to practice discernment from a particular location, namely,
the confession that God is the active agent shaping the realities we confront. This means that we must confront the defaults of management and
control that signify, fundamentally, a functional atheism.

A Christian imagination does not read what is happening off the latest
sociocultural, political-economic or technological-media frameworks.
The church's primary responses come from a biblical and theological
framing that continually re-presents the fact of God's agency. We reimagine what it means to be God's people in this strange, new space, first,
by seeing God as the active agent in the midst of all this disruption. Such
a stance compels us to ask how we discern the movement of the Spirit in
order to understand what God is up to in the disruptions. Throughout
Israel's story in the Old Testament and those of the church through its
history, the Spirit continually disrupts the settled life of God's people,
pushing them out of established frameworks and boundaries in order to
compel them to reframe their lives to be more faithfully a sign, witness
and foretaste of the kingdom. Throughout these engagements, the Spirit
is the primary agent, thrusting God's people (most of the time unwill-
ingly) into unknown, unmanageable spaces where by reentering founding
stories, which involves a wrestling with legitimating narratives, new
imagination and practices emerge. This is what is happening in Moses'
engagement with God and with Israel in the desert.

For the Eurotribal churches to perceive their disorienting, disruptive
realities primarily in terms of sociocultural, economic-political or global-
izing explanations is to limit their discernment to the dominant explanations of our time. In the midst of all these realities the Christian confession and imagination is that God is the primary active agent in the

world, and the Spirit is the primary actor in the midst of all that is oc-curring. To discern this unraveling from a Christian perspective is to see that the Spirit has propelled the Eurotribal churches into spaces where they have not been before in order to invite them to join God's transfor-mation of the world. Other accountings are secondary and derivative from this perspective. How are these churches to dwell in this new space? What structures and practices are required?

The disruptive actions of the Spirit are not intended to leave us pow-erless. The resurrection gives us a critical frame for a Christian imagi-nation. Concretized in the resurrection is the fact that God is the primary agent in the midst of massively disruptive events that cannot be fit into our existing categories of meaning or expected actions. This does not mean that God wills these events but that in the midst of them God is actively present, as with Israel in Egypt, to invite God's people into an as-yet-unseen future. The biblical narratives are formed in an escha-tology—God's movement in, for and with the world toward a future. No organizational system or its leadership can manage, control, encapsulate or program the Spirit's disruptive future.

A number of implications of God's agency follow. First, the Spirit's disruptions are into spaces that cannot be planned for or strategized from the perspective of the previous context. Second, being primarily focused on applying existing, normative skills and frameworks will usually mis-direct us from discerning what God is doing. Third, existing methods organizations use to engage challenges are largely untenable in this new space. Fourth, a basic change in the imaginative frameworks around which people have been operating is essential. Fifth, this new imagi-native framework won't fit inside existing ways of operating. Sixth, dis-cerning these frameworks requires experimentation. Several examples will help clarify this.

Prior to the Babylonian Captivity, the people of Jerusalem (including its primary leadership) settled into patterns that assumed how God was present among them. These assumptions enabled them to develop orga-nizational structures rooted in the conviction that God was on their side and Jerusalem was the center of God's activity. They were, therefore, eruptively decentered from this world (hardly anyone, including the leadership, saw it coming). Because the system of life in Jerusalem and the roles of its leaders were embedded in assumptions of domain, command and control, the loss of Jerusalem was seen as a gargantuan calamity that had to be fixed, rather than a sign of the disruptive agency of God's Spirit. Disruption was a problem to be solved, not an invitation to a new imagination. Babylon put the people in a situation where their assumptions about being God's people were turned upside down. There could be no business as usual in Babylon. Applying the practices and strategies of Jerusalem could not help the captives make sense of the situation. They needed a different imagination. Resistance to this interpretation of God's activities was high. Many sought for a return.

A similar example of the Spirit's disruptive dynamic is seen in the boundary-breaking challenges shaping Acts. After Pentecost the church quickly assumed the existing practices of Judaism and temple worship. It organized around this imagination, creating rules and regulations for a Jewish-Christian church (e.g., dietary laws and circumcision). Jesus' community would live within Judaism. Unexpectedly, the Spirit shattered these assumptions. Through persecution and the agency of unknown disciples crossing sociocultural and ethnic boundaries (Antioch), the face of the Christian movement was transformed in ways that had not entered the imagination of those in Jerusalem at Pentecost.

The organizational and leadership assumptions that shaped Judaism in Jerusalem could not contain this disruptive, boundary-breaking work of the Spirit. The transformation was stunning. Little in the narrative formation of leaders prepared them for this sudden metamorphosis. The acts of unknown disciples driven by the Spirit did not come from assumed scripts. These actions could not be codified into the existing structures.

The Spirit's disrupting of established patterns results in several effects. First, as the Babylon and Jerusalem narratives suggest, in disruptive change the default to existing organizational forms and the legitimating narratives that underlie them act as dampers to discerning the Spirit's actions. The churches default to existing organizational practices that focus attention on programs (revitalization) or outcome-based strategies (new sets of goals or dashboards). Second, the power of these defaults means that the churches fail to recognize that the disrupting of the Spirit is actually a sign God isn't finished with them. There remains work to be done, but it can only be discerned from outside the existing imagination. It can't be engaged from within those current narratives that provide identity, security and success. How, then, can the denominations thrive in these places where they've never been before?

The challenges before these denominations are significant. How to fund national programs? How to form leaders when full-time clergy have become a luxury fewer congregations can afford? How to engage the plurality of narratives inviting the attention and loyalty of church members? What is the nature of justice in a multiperspectival world? Where do emerging generations engage? Amid all this, how can denominations resist the power of default solutions (e.g., new programs for disciple-making, a strategy to revitalize congregations based on growth metrics, another method of training with a redesigned, online MDiv)? The predisposition is to look for solutions inside established methods.

The challenge is to take the time to understand the level of work to be done in changing the defaults. Ronald Heifetz and Marty Linsky describe this as "getting on the balcony" to see what is happening on the dance floor.[2] Balcony work looks to see our organization's functional defaults and our own implications in them. In this place it's possible to ask the questions of what other narratives and imagination will be required to reframe the church's life. Such a posture enables us to discern the actual defaults shaping our actions, which is part of cultivating a new imagination.

IMAGINATION AND GOD'S DISRUPTIVE TIME

Imagination is more than a list of new ideas. It's not about dreams or vision statements. It's about how we see the world (hence the metaphor of the balcony). This involves the metaphors and stories that determine how we believe the world works and the nature of our role within it. In the midst of the Spirit's disruptions is this invitation to reimagine how our denominational systems work. The narrative imagination of the churches described in part one resulted in powerful defaults that remain at play across all levels of the churches (local, regional and national). The next section looks at these defaults as a precursor to proposing a way forward.

What are defaults? Researching this question immediately illustrates their power. It is an interesting commentary on our time to note that the default definition of *default* in a quick Google search is some form of failure on a financial obligation, as in defaulting on a mortgage. It illustrates just how deeply economic frameworks are the default way of reading our world. In the European debt crisis countries like Greece, Italy and Spain are discovering that the primary interpretive framework for determining the directions of a country is no longer the political decisions of democratically elected officials but the dictates of the market. This is an illustration of a powerful default lying just beneath the surface of everything we do. It provides a simple illustration of the power of defaults on how we see the world. This hegemony of money and commerce is the definitive imagination running in the background and determining how we read our world. But there are many others.

In this book *default* refers to the way in which systems (natural, social and mechanical) build into themselves taken-for-granted explanatory frameworks that kick into place and predetermine actions. A car, for example, has a built-in default that cause its brakes to come on and off in a skid-avoidance pattern. A clam closes its shell as a perceived predator comes too close. Our body has built-in defaults to produce antibodies when it senses attack. Defaults are the internalized habits, practices, attitudes and values individuals or social systems use to read and navigate actions in their environment. They are the taken-for-granted ways we've worked out over time to get things done. This is one of the reasons focusing primarily on organizational and structural change actually fails to bring about substantive change. Organizational and structural changes (e.g., redefining roles of leaders) don't address underlying defaults.

In Babylon the default of the deported Jews involved strategies for returning to Jerusalem. Despite clear instructions from God (Jer 29) to remain in the city that had caused such devastation, their default was to return to what they knew—the familiarity of Jerusalem with its known places and symbols of normalcy. Beneath this default there lay an imagination that said God could only be properly known back in Jerusalem under certain kinds of operations and with certain types of leaders. There was little capacity to imagine or discern that God was in fact shaping a very different story. The defaults were so powerful that most could only read the captivity within the frameworks of return. In a similar manner, immediately after Pentecost the default assumption of the disciples was a temple-based life centered in Jerusalem. Similarly, denominational systems (national, regional and local) today continue to operate out of defaults formed in the twentieth century, which cause them to bring established responses and proposals to the disruptive changes they face.

Learning to see defaults and understand how they work helps us begin to frame alternative imaginations. It isn't an easy task. When the Spirit disrupts established categories, this creates a resistance that triggers our defaults. Changing imagination is about changing defaults. To a large extent imagination is about the metaphors we use to describe who we are and how we engage our contexts. Sometimes, we are able to see and reflect on these metaphors. This can be observed, for example, in the language people use to describe who they are as a group. Ask a congregation, for example, for words that describe how they see themselves and many will immediate use the word *family*. Family is a metaphor that encapsulates a congregation's collective imagination about itself. A metaphor is never neutral. It determines how we will relate to one another (within the family) and how we respond to those outside (the nonfamily, so to speak). Family is about closely bound blood relationship. Transferred to a congregation it gradually results in a gathering of people focused in on itself and the kinds of relationships they might or might not have with one another within the family.

Metaphors are powerful shapers of imagination. When they are as obvious and self-consciously named as the family image, they can be addressed by holding up the language to the mirror of self-reflection and inviting people to work on the implications of this language for the kinds of decisions they are making, the programs they are developing and how they see people outside the family. But many of the metaphors that are most determinative to church life at this moment are not so obvious. The majority of them, in fact, function at a precritical, taken-for-granted level.

PRECRITICAL METAPHORS AND THE DISRUPTIONS OF THE SPIRIT

The ways denominations have shaped their organizational life expresses their underlying convictions about how the world works. These convictions are formed out of specific metaphors that feed and structure the organizational life of that system. Therefore, they shape how members are trained, skills are developed and identity is given.

These precritical metaphors determine not just actions but emotional responses to change. Like an operating system running in the background, they are continually determining how an organization sees the world, the actions it chooses and the sources of its sense of worth in the world. They shape how an organization responds to disruptive change. They run under the radar. They're not driven by stated theological convictions or denominational distinctives (note, for example, the similarity of organizational structures across denominations with different theologies and polities). They determine how these theologies and polities are played out in everyday life.

As the Spirit disrupts the churches into spaces where established leadership and organizational skills, status and abilities are dislocated, the precritical metaphors must be attended to. In disruptive contexts default metaphors kick in with a vengeance, directing us to engage disruptive space with existing models. Leaders in churches and denominational systems under duress work harder at applying their default skills, practices, habits and structures out of these underlying metaphors because this has been their zone of comfort and professional identity. These defaults are what have made them successful to this point. National bodies, for example, do research studies (with surveys and other forms of information gathering) to gather data on such issues as decline of youth involvement, dwindling membership rolls or managing fewer resources. From the data they design programs, determine actions and establish communications procedures to inform and invite people across the system to join them in their new initiatives. This approach is endemic in organizational systems developed in the twentieth century. In cities, for instance, as roadways get clogged with increased traffic, the default is to build more roads. What has become increasingly clear in urban planning is that building more roads does not solve the problem of congestion. The widened highway, for example, very quickly becomes clogged again as more people drive on the road. The answers have to be found in alternative directions. When power grids can't produce sufficient electricity to meet demand, the default response is to build more massive power generators. This will be discussed later in terms of Germany's decision to build more nuclear plants for power generation in the face of uncertainty from oil and gas costs and delivery. The default decision to build more power generators came out of deeply embedded defaults that will be illustrated in the coming chapters. Established defaults tend to control how organizations respond to challenges that can't be addressed without a fundamental change of imagination. Established defaults read disruptive challenges as variants of established patterns.

Defaults don't disappear because an organization declares they will change or create some new structure through which to operate. Defaults go deep into the DNA, continuing to shape habits, attitudes, practices and values long after they have been declared finished. This leads to a discussion of the default imagination that continues to shape the denominations, their leaders and their churches.

8

The Hub and Spoke

HUB AND SPOKE

An underlying metaphor shaping the default approach of denominational systems is a specific organizational model called hub and spoke. This imagination still shapes their responses to disruptive change even while there is much discussion about being in a new space, or recognition that new processes must be implemented. Again, this is not about what people think they are doing or the kinds of decisions they claim they are making—it is about the underlying social imaginaries.

The next sections summarize the basic tenets of this imagination, explaining how it works and where it is creating growing levels of anxiety, misunderstanding and conflict. While once effective in driving the life of denominations, it has ceased to provide a meaningful way of engaging their changed sociocultural environments. As Wittgenstein so pithily stated: "A picture held us captive. And we couldn't get outside of it, for it lay in our language, and language seemed only to repeat it to us inexorably."[1]

The hub and spoke metaphor continues to shape how denominations operate, how decisions are made and how strategies for change are developed. While an adaptable organizational model, the hub-spoke default presents significant challenges to the kind of imaginative shift required of denominations.

Figure 8.1 illustrates the basic imagination. The wheel is an amazing invention that radically changed human life. As an imaginative framing of how to make "the world go round," it lies deep in our operational metaphors. The bicycle wheel, for example, has a center and a periphery with spokes connecting each. This basic design becomes a powerful technology for doing many things very effectively. The model is based on a center-periphery design. As an organizational model it functions within a movement, back and forth, between center and periphery. In the case of denominations in the twentieth century, this movement was from national through regional to local. This has been a basic social imaginary for all kinds of organizational structures (profit and nonprofit) through most of the twentieth century. It underlay the functioning of the corporate denomination, whose defaults and practices continue to shape denominational interactions and planning. This might be called the traditional or standard organizational design in the sense that it is the environment in which most current national and regional leaders of denominations were formed.

The classic hub and spoke organizational structure works as a hierarchy that maximizes efficiencies through management (by objectives) and control (of outcomes). It has been a centralized organizational structure populated by experts and professionals through a division of labor (series of departments) that determines what is needed for those at the periphery of the hub in terms of resources and programs.[2] The hub designs what its experts and studies determine is needed, and then it disseminates them across the spokes toward the peripheries. In the twentieth

Figure 8.1. Hub-spoke

century this became a unipolar organizational structure that viewed the hub (through its professionals, experts and endless studies) as best situated to provide the research, resources and personnel required to create an integrated strategy for addressing change. As denominational systems grew, intermediary units such as presbyteries, regions, conferences, synods, dioceses and so forth became mediating structures along the spokes for distributing the goods and services down the spokes to the peripheries. This default imagination prevailed even though the theological confessions of some denominations were rooted in the autonomy of the local church and a commitment to a so-called bottom-up process.

As a primary organizational imagination, hub-spoke structure is not tenable in disruptive environments requiring adaptive recalibration of organizational imagination and functionality. Denominations can no longer resource or lead from an imagination of being at the center in relationship to regions and local contexts. While leaders across the denominations recognize this, they have not understood how this powerful hub-spoke default operates in the background like software predetermining actions. The past decades have witnessed denominations moving through restructuring processes whereby national responsibilities were offloaded to the regional and local as part of budget, personnel and program reductions. Concurrently, a cyclical series of reorganizations took place with little if any reflection on the underlying dynamic of this

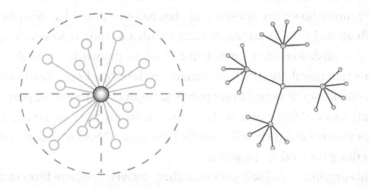

Figure 8.2. Offloading down the spoke

controlling hub-spoke default. In most of these processes the basic metaphor/imagination informing denominational actions has remained a hub to spoke, center to periphery imagination. Figure 8.2 illustrates some of the ways denominations have offloaded down the spoke without recognizing the continuing power of the basic metaphor.

In each case the basic metaphor of a central hub continues to determine actions and outcomes. In organizational change and restructuring, this metaphor remains even while trying to build in structures of interaction and feedback. Beneath new programming, restructuring and the proclaiming of interactive, networked relationships, this default metaphor remains in place. This means that in the midst of the dislocating change unraveling denominations, efforts to address this new space fail because all the good work at national and midlevel judicatories is being grafted onto this underlying default. The result is increasing discouragement toward and resistance to national and midlevel judicatories. New pilot projects and proposals increasingly find themselves confronting skeptical terrain. Some further background to this reality will help us see more clearly what is at stake.

ENDING OF THE AGE OF THE CORPORATE DENOMINATION

We cannot capture in simple statements the complex disruptions now reframing denominations. The twentieth century was largely characterized by the corporate denomination. Craig Van Gelder uses the metaphor of DNA to explain how denominations have unique characteristics determining how they operate and change over time.[3] He describes denominational DNA as an "organization with a purposive intent designed to accomplish something on behalf of God in the world."[4] On the basis of this functional identity, denominations developed organizational self-understandings designed to support and implement this basic purposive intent. Van Gelder's point is that denominations have organized themselves to carry out their self-identified purpose (DNA) of accomplishing something for God in the world.

This organizational self-understanding is given concrete form in structures shaped by underlying convictions about how to implement their purposive intent most effectively. Through most of the twentieth century that organizational structure was some form of the corporate denomination. Underlying that structure (head offices, regions/conferences/areas/dioceses, and local congregations/parishes) was the hub-spoke default metaphor, which was like a piece of DNA determining how decisions were made, where they were made and the ways actions were carried out.

Organizational forms are not neutral, and the corporate denomination carried its own implicit narrative about how the world was meant to work in terms of efficiency, management and expertise. Organizational structures are a function of imagination, metaphors functioning as basic convictions about how purposive intent is achieved in the world. In the twentieth century denominations were built on a core genetic code that sought to maximize productivity and efficiency across their organizations. To do this they adopted a center-periphery (hub and spoke) structure based on expertise, professionalization and command-and-control within a hierarchical bureaucracy. It remains the background metaphor informing decisions in denominations even in the midst of disruptive change.

The genius of hub and spoke is how it provided effective organizational structure for both the context and values of thriving denominational systems right into its last quarter of the twentieth century, when it unraveled. While this unraveling became critical at the beginning of the new millennium, the hub-spoke imagination continues to influence decision making. Some basic assumptions of this default imagination are:

1. It assumes the expert has the greatest information and knowledge about specific areas or skills. The hub is built on expertise.

2. The most efficient way for an organization to function is by efficiently centralizing expertise and resources. In Valley Forge, Indianapolis, Nashville and New York, large, centralized headquarters sprang up as the hubs of the cradle-to-grave, corporate denomination.

3. From the hub, spokes radiate efficiently, carrying expertise and resources out to regional and local settings. This is generally one-way communication where experts study peripheries, determining what resources and expertise need to be housed at the hub and sent down the spokes to end users.

4. Effective design of programs and resources requires the confluence of skill, expertise and resources in a centralized location.

5. Managing large geographies requires intermediary structures (conferences, regions or presbyteries) along the spokes, like electrical transfer stations, where subgroups of experts, more accessible to the peripheries, distribute the resources along the supply line. The point here is that the intermediating structures are carrying or transferring the center's operational life out to its peripheries. The challenge is to

imagine how structures such as presbyteries, conferences, dioceses and so forth shift from being primarily intermediary structures between a center and a periphery to become centers for distributive learning communities (clusters of congregations) learning ways of being agents of God's mission in adaptive spaces.

The hub-spoke imagination is firmly in place. Such metaphors are not like clothes that can be discarded once fashion changes. They produce deeply embedded habits and practices that shape the imagination of those inside organizational structures over extended periods of time. They are the hidden defaults that continue to drive the operations of an organization even when there is sufficient information to show they can no longer address the existing situation. The hub-spoke continues to inform the decision makers and the experts in denominations even while they are able to state that the age of the corporate denomination is past. The following examples from actual situations in 2010-2011 illustrate how powerful these defaults remain.

A local church. More than twenty years ago a young pastor arrived at a small church. Through continual expository preaching and the development of effective children's, youth and adult ministries, the church grew and added staff in an upper-middle-class context. The growing staff ran its multiple programs as part of a full-service church, offering something to meet the needs of people across the community. The senior pastor continued to preach well and manage a full-blown set of cradle-to-grave services for the church. Over the past five years significant transformations are shaking the confidence of the upper-middle-class people attending this church. A palpable sense of anxiety and disquiet has grown as people face the loss of jobs they thought recession-proof. Companies are not only laying people off and off-shoring work, but cutting retirement benefits and no longer providing the assumed yearly salary increase.

Something is happening in a society that seemed well ordered. These educated leaders, church members and experts of society find themselves, for the first time in their lives, in a place where their explanations no longer explain and their actions no longer fix. The anxiety spills over into the church. It is felt among people, but most keenly noticed in the gradual curve downward of both attendance and giving. This, in turn, creates another kind of anxiety for pastoral staff (their jobs) and especially the senior pastor, who is asking, "What am I doing wrong when everything I have done in the past has worked so well, but it's not producing the same results today?" The senior pastor feels the need to act. He is the primary leader of the church. People have looked up to him all these years; he now needs to come up with answers. In the midst of these stressors, the denomination he has belonged to all his life is going through its own clash of values and convictions. Issues of sexuality and ordination have preoccupied the denomination for years. As anxieties rise, it seems the denomination has reached a breaking point where decisions must be made. This combination of factors shapes the senior pastor's decisions. He gathers his staff and instructs them to design more effective programs of discipleship and stewardship. He meets with his official board in order to set the church onto a road of conversation about its future in the denomination. A new level of energy emerges in the senior pastor and staff as they are focused on actions, the development of programs and the sense they are acting righteously in making the congregation choose to leave the denomination.

This senior pastor and the congregation face significant stressors. In the midst of massive sociocultural upheavals many in the congregation feel that their lives are being turned upside down by forces they no longer understand and pressures they never expected. Beneath the surface of polite conversation, Bible study, small groups and voluntarism in programs runs a deep disease that preaching and programs no longer address. The senior pastor defaults to patterns that produced a successful past until recently. He applies the hub-spoke structure with his staff functioning as experts to address the issues he sees (disciples and stewardship) while missing the deeper issues of identity and meaning in disruptive social contexts. He deflects energy from the hard, underlying questions that he has no answers for by focusing the church on a discussion of its leaving the denomination for one more faithful to his set of theological assumptions.

National denomination A. A national denomination wrestles with a series of indisputable factors about a long decline. Over a forty-year period it has lost 50 percent of its membership. While the percentage of yearly decline has slowed, numbers continue to trend down. No matter what ruler or dashboard is used, the metrics point toward an implosion in a relatively short time. Something must be done. Denominational leaders (in this case, bishops) see the need to act decisively. They mandate a national study of the church across the country, involving demographics and focus groups around what makes a church vital. On the basis of this data they develop criteria based on the vital congregation research mandating a series of actions congregations and their leaders must take to become vital. These include using the metrics of numerical growth projections and church attendance over a twelve-month period. The national meeting of the bishops mandates this be a national program resourced by a national staff at the central office.

Leaders of this denomination are appropriately aware of the critical challenges confronting their churches. They are determined to take action to address these challenges. In so doing, the social imaginary of a hub-spoke structure operates as the dominant narrative. They worked with a centralized decision-making process that they mandated down the spokes.

National denomination B. A national denomination is structured around separate operational groups with differing functionalities developed more than a century ago. They have separate and independent organizations for national (home) ministries and international (overseas) ministries (other denominations follow similar patterns for women, youth, church planting, ethnic ministries, etc.). Though the world that created this organizational imagination no longer exists, the denomination continues to function in this way. Each agency works in a silo, with its own staff, experts, programs and funding sources (or competition for the same diminishing sources of funding).

As funding sources decline, these organizations face major challenges to their capacity to fund existing programs. Boards are requiring their staffs to make cost-saving program and staff cuts. Local congregations, as membership profiles age, can't give the dollars they once did. Others no longer see the benefit of national bodies, questioning their purpose and functionality while diverting monies to local ministries or directly to mission in other countries.

National organizations are responding to the disruptions within the hub-spoke imagination by mandating studies of programs, resources and staffing. They carry out exhaustive focus-group studies resulting in reports and recommendations from experts. On this basis new priorities are developed around which staff will operate and resources are assigned. Staff initiate recalibrated programs. From within the existing social imaginary such actions make sense. Yet they won't address disruptive change or the loss of confidence in national bodies.

Despite the best of intentions on the part of national staffs and their boards, the processes summarized here demonstrate how they continue to function out of hub-spoke and center-periphery structural defaults. This is not about the desire or intentionality of national leaders, but the underlying metaphor determining actions and outcomes. Such actions will not connect with the actual on-the-ground challenges being faced by the churches.

CULTURE CHANGE: ENERGY AND INERTIA

Megan McArdle observes, "Even a dysfunctional culture, once well established, is astonishingly efficient at reproducing itself."[5] Before moving to proposing ways forward, it is important to return to the section in part one that focused on culture change.[6] The argument made throughout part one is that organizational structures and roles express deeper cultural narratives (social imaginaries). Defaults and metaphors operate at the level of culture that is the precritical and taken-for-granted way a group reads its world. The primary challenge for the denominations at every level of their life, therefore, is to engage in culture change rather than simply to work harder at the organizational, structural and role issues.

Culture is hard to change. It takes time, patience, persistence and different skills from the expertise, management and control of the hub-spoke. In a helpful reflection on why companies fail, McArdle reflects on the failure and supposed comeback of General Motors following its 2008 implosion.[7] Her reflections bear up our discussion about culture and denominational renewal. She reflects on the fact that post-2008 and GM's bailout, externally, the company has done a lot of things right. That being said, there are many signs that it may not have actually changed its deeper corporate culture. She paraphrases an old joke that is restated here in terms of denominations rather than GM: "How many experts does it take to turn around a denomination? Only one—but the denomination has to really want to change."

McArdle points to more underlying questions about the culture of organizations facing significant challenges. She provides the following quote from Paul Ingrassia's 2010 book, *Crash Course*:

> Throughout the 1980s and 1990s, every time the Big Three and the UAW returned to prosperity, they would succumb to hubris and lapse back into their old bad habits. It was like a Biblical cycle of repentance, reform, and going astray, again and again, as Detroit was repeatedly lured by the golden calves of corporate excess and union overreach. The cycle reached its peak at the beginning of the new millennium, when the Big Three plunged from record profits to breathtaking losses in just five years.

McArdle's point is not whether the Big Three have made significant and tough decisions about remaking themselves; it's whether the underlying cultural narratives have actually been addressed.

One way of getting at this question is through the dual roles of energy and inertia. At the level of activities in terms of refinancing, managing union relations and pension plans, or coming up with new designs for cars, it is clear that GM has put a huge amount of energy into change. On the other hand, there's the question of inertia, which is about an organization's underlying DNA (remember Van Gelder's descriptions of denominations). An organization can put huge amounts of energy into functional and tactical change (battery-driven cars, leaner operating budgets through the use of robots, and reductions in pension payouts) while not addressing the underlying DNA (its culture).

Why is this the case? It's not because people are afraid of change. This is not a satisfactory explanation. A better explanation goes to the way DNA works. Using this metaphor to describe an organization, such as a denomination, it may be the case that inertia is about the organization's DNA—it has developed genes that have made it successful and therefore provided it with a high level of legitimacy in the society. But as the environment goes through massive transformation, those genes now do the opposite; they are causing the organization to fail. This is the situation described previously in terms of operating defaults. It's about culture and culture change. All the studies about buying habits around automobiles (or church attendance) will not address this deeper issue of DNA. Energy at one level gives short-term (eighteen to twenty-four month) upswings, but then the system goes back to business as usual because this activity does not address the inertia which functions at the other level (DNA).

Culture change is hard for a number of reasons. First, it really does require some level of leap into the unknown, and that is risky. It involves doing something that people probably haven't done before. Current experts, professionals and leaders will have little sense of how it's all going to work out (one of Heifetz's main points about the nature of adaptive change). That requires a big imaginative shift.

In one denominational system, the leader of a midlevel judicatory expressed resistance to using a process for effecting culture change. Some of the reasons for this resistance were legitimate, but one illustrates this point of change and the risk of the unknown. The executive kept pushing back onto us the question of outcomes. He wanted to know what the results would be, what were the measurables. These questions were asked numerous times, as if they represented an implicit argument against the processes we were proposing.

At some point in the discussion he began to describe the challenges faced by his judicatory over the past fifty years. He described eloquently the continued upheavals faced by the churches as they confronted waves of immigrant communities from other countries with differing languages, cultures and religions. He talked about the economic and social challenges these churches were confronted with over this half-century period. In this description he was expressing pride in the ways the people of these churches had risked and experimented in the midst of continually changing environments. He was unable to see the connection between these stories and the invitation to enter a similar imaginative space to address the new challenges confronting his churches and the denomination. His stories described people willing to leap into the unknown and do things they hadn't done before. At the beginning, the people of these churches had no sense of how it would all work out, but they experimented and in so doing learned to change key elements of their DNA. But in the context of his own critical struggles with a changed environment, he was asking for clear outcomes and results. We are averse to change that invites us to risk outside what we know.

Second, organizations like predictability. McArdle gives the illustration of McDonald's, with its commitment that wherever a person goes, everything in the restaurant will be exactly the same as in other McDonald's restaurants. A number of years ago I was in China working with a number of churches. One evening our Chinese hosts took us North Americans out for supper, treating us to a wide assortment of Chinese food that definitely is not found on the menu of the local Chinese food take out. As these exotic dishes were passed around on the lazy Susan, one of my North American companions turned and asked with utter seriousness about where she could find the closest McDonald's. As soon as supper was over, she headed out of the door to get her supper at McDonald's. No matter how critical we might view the situation in our denominations, the inner need for predictability is so strong that we default to what we know rather than embrace risk in places we have never been before. It's much more comfortable to do one more study, develop yet another set of dashboards and outcomes, and then initiate yet another program than enter a world where none of this makes sense.

Third, culture change is hard because when conditions in the environment change, our thinking doesn't. During periods of stability and predictability in the larger sociocultural environment, such as the denominations in the first three quarters of the twentieth century, organizations can put a lot of energy into programmatic and developmental work while basically ignoring internal dysfunction. The fact that externally there is success and most elements of the denomination's work are going relatively well (growth in numbers or financial commitments, investments providing healthy returns, etc.) removes the impetus to deal with some of the underlying dysfunctions in the culture of the organization. Examples of this abound.

In some denominational headquarters various divisions became deeply siloed, each protecting its shop from the other, each managing its own domain with little more than a head nod to what was happening in the other silos. As long as there was apparent success in the expected metrics, and monies flowed in through giving or endowments, no one bothered with these dysfunctions. Some denominations, for example, failed to develop a culture of gift development and fundraising outside of national giving formulas. When the larger environment changed (congregational decline, competition for dwindling dollars, loss of loyalty to national bodies, loss of identity to denominational brands), national and regional organizations began to implode, and the underlying, internal dysfunctions became hugely problematic. In one denomination the trust levels eroded between national and midlevel judicatories to the point where each blamed and accused the other in myriad ways. One could sit with a midlevel executive who would immediately begin a litany of blame toward national offices. The anger and mistrust was deep. The learned practices had created a culture of complaint. On the other side, one would sit with national staff, and they would quickly move into their own blame game using the language of "them" to describe midlevel leadership, followed by their own litany of why "they" were the problem, why "they" didn't appreciate or support the work of these national staff. Each group moved into its own siloed world while politely meeting with the other at national events but never addressing the elephant in the room. Each had its own email loops reinforcing the dysfunctional culture of complaint.

None of this mattered that much when the money came in and the systems grew. Now that those days are gone and the hard realities of culture change stare these groups in the face, the dysfunctions, operating at this level of culture, become massive obstacles to the reimagining of denominational life. As McArdle states, "Even a dysfunctional culture, once well established, is astonishingly efficient at reproducing itself."[8] It's not about the structures—it's about the culture! Chapter nine addresses the culture changes denominations will need to make.

Changing the Culture of
the Denominations

*An approach would be to simply pick up the tools at
hand, begin building the solutions, and pull
more people and larger jurisdictions
into the project as you go along.*

Chris Turner, *The Leap*

THE DISTRIBUTIVE AGE

If you travel a great deal, the question of luggage is not unimportant. How should you efficiently manage the endless duty of carrying your tightly packed belongings from one plane to another, from taxi to hotel to taxi? It all seems too simple these days, but it wasn't always so. Not long ago, a simple act of imagination revolutionized travel. Someone broke the mold by deciding to do the uncommon—put wheels on luggage. The rest is history! But note what occurred. This wasn't radical restructuring. No one broke the suitcase; rather, they had a different imagination about how to make the suitcase work. It really is the little things that count in culture change.

The economies of countries like China and India continue to grow at incredible rates. This produces new challenges. How, for example, can India, a vast country, provide electricity (which is a primary engine of economic growth) to the millions of people who live in very poor conditions? Addressing this critical challenge from the perspective of existing imagination, such as building multiple new, huge electrical generation plants, is out of the question. What then can be done with this urgent need for energy in the myriad locales beyond large cities? Why not provide small loans to poor people developing their own micro-businesses? This will enable households to install small, simple, efficient solar panels on their roofs. This simple shift in imagination that works with existing, small-scale housing is changing the way thousands of people are able to imagine their place in the new economy. Again, it is not about some radical reorganization or the development of mega-projects. Rather, such change is about seeing what already exists from a different perspective that creates imagination and innovation at the local level. The point being made here is that in times of significant adaptive cultural change, large, centralized organizational and structural change is not the solution. Bishop Graham Cray, a friend with whom I have had many conversations, describes how this was understood in key parts of the Church of England and resulted in the development of Fresh Expressions as a process of seeding and energizing imagination and experiments at the local level. *Culture change in adaptive environments is about cultivating among people at the local level the capacities to reimagine and experiment.*

The crisis confronting denominations is one of imagination. What is required is a revolution in imagination that enables us to move away from established cultural metaphors (such as hub-spoke). We are no longer in a period of management and predictability (where the shape of the immediate future is fairly predictable because it will probably be continuous with the immediate past) that allowed us to create centralized operations run by experts (where programs were dreamed up by teams of professionals and then marketed down the chain).[1] We live in what is being called a "distributive age." It is a time that calls for cooperation in which ideas are generated at the local level and experimentation cultivates an alternative future. *This distributive age does not call for the dismantling of existing structures but the investment of trust in very different places.* It is within this imagination of a distributive age that denominational systems will discover the elements of culture and DNA change they have to address. In order to explain the nature of this distributive imagination, we will turn to some of the reimagining happening in other sectors of Western life.

ELECTRIC COMPANIES AND IMAGINATION

The challenge of culture change is not unique to denominations. Recently, we had friends visiting us from the United Kingdom. Martin and Linda Robinson live in Birmingham and have codeveloped a missional leadership training program that has caught hold across the UK.[2] Linda was describing to us how her brother, a building contractor, had just purchased a German-made home that is, in effect, its own generator of electricity and has a continuous water supply. Behind this innovation lies a story of how Germany has, over the past decade, shifted from dependence on fossil fuels to a radically different imagination for meeting its energy needs. This is a story that relates to the emergence of this distributive age. Project Edison in Denmark is also an illustration of this distributive movement.[3]

Electric companies in Western nations were created around classic hub-spoke organizational models. Some of the reasons for this are very practical and make a good deal of sense. Their structure was rooted in the confluence of factors that came together and worked extremely well in the nineteenth and twentieth centuries. First, those creating these companies saw what appeared at the time as an endless source of nonrenewable energy in the form of oil, coal, natural gas and water. Electric companies established themselves as centralized, hub-spoke management organizations adjacent to the cheap, abundant natural resources (water, coal, oil and, later, nuclear plants) they were exploiting. While the generation of power was therefore usually far away from the endpoints it was delivered to, it was economically feasible to construct extensive, though expensive, infrastructures in the form of transmission lines and substations because the abundance of cheap natural resources and the subsidies of governments produced significant profits for these companies.

The ready availability of an abundant resource (or its closeness to the transportation systems developed to deliver the resource) determined location. From this central generating location (hub) an electrical company hung thousands of miles of transmission lines (spokes) carrying electricity to peripheries (factories, homes, commercial businesses, etc.). The hub-spoke electrical grid is today one of the most taken-for-granted structures of energy production and delivery. All down the line, from extraction to generation to delivery, it is a one-way, increasingly expensive infrastructure dependent on high levels of cheap, nonrenewable fuel, cheap transportation (massively subsidized by governments) and large numbers of end users. As demand rose through the last century and competition grew for cheap energy (and then just energy), the challenge of producing and delivering electricity became acute.

The basic, underlying metaphor (hub and spoke) functioned as an internal default for experts, professionals, politicians and the public. Practically everyone assumed that (1) more generating stations would need to be developed, attached to sources of energy and delivered great distances by power lines, and (2) there would be greater and greater needs for conservation in order to reduce the growing costs to end users. Germany, for example, determined by the beginning of the new millennium it would have to bring online a considerable number of new nuclear plants. Some of the reasons for this decision were (1) the escalating costs of oil and gas, (2) the political instability of the Middle East, and (3) the fragility of relations with Russia, from which Germany exported most of its gas. Each of these factors contributed to a massive adaptive challenge to the industrial production of Germany. The decision to develop nuclear plants is an illustration of a classical hub-spoke imagination. Few could imagine any other alternative to the conventional hub-spoke responses requiring large, increasingly expensive, centralized hierarchies managing the system at every step down the line. Large numbers of focus-group studies, research into the use of electricity at varying times and data on the expectations of people for electrical use in the coming decades were carried out inside this dominant metaphor. The proposed solutions, therefore, remained embedded within this imagination, and all decisions were made on the basis of its optimization. Indeed, all proposals to address electrical needs from outside this corporate, hub-spoke hierarchy were derided as the impractical dreams of people who didn't understand the issues and had no experience of the realities.

Countries with scarce quantities of nonrenewable fuel resources were at the front side of an economic and social crisis as they felt the pressure of costs from purchasing oil or coal offshore. They were in an increasingly difficult place and needed to find alternatives as the costs of imports (oil, coal, etc.) climbed skyward. This pressure accelerated the search for alternatives. The obvious place to turn was the renewable sector with its use of wind turbines and solar energy. But when experts in the field of energy, and politicians facing the electorate's demands for stability, predictability and a solution to high energy prices, looked at the alternatives, all they saw were the reasons why renewables could never work. The claim was made that renewables were not scalable to the levels of production required and estimated into the immediate future. The accepted perception was that they were not dependable (wind and sun are intermittent, especially in northern regions). The numbers of units (windmills and solar panels) required to make the system work would be astronomical and utterly unaffordable. The general consensus from those within electrical industry, the politicians, the media and the general public was that renewables were at best a marginal answer to the electrical needs of late industrial societies and, in the main, a pipe dream! In other words, there was little capacity to imagine alternatives outside dominant defaults.

These diverse groups came to this conclusion for a primary reason—the experts in energy production (i.e., electrical production) had all been trained in the hub-spoke imagination because that was practically the only form of energy production that functioned within these countries. There were few, if any, alternatives, and those that existed were small and ineffective. The people running the power companies and the consultants to the politicians were all formed within and trained with a hub-spoke world, because that was the world of electrical generation. All debate and calculations (metrics and dashboards) were built around the assumptions of the hub-spoke imagination. Few realized this was the unspoken, driving paradigm predetermining how people saw what was at stake. But what if there was a different imagination?

What if a different set of metrics based on alternative metaphors shaped the imagination for addressing these challenges? It might dramatically reframe the conversation! This imagination was present. It would require risk, stepping outside powerful, taken-for-granted defaults to discern a way forward that was counterintuitive.

This other imagination had to do with asking questions in a different way. What if, instead of asking about the generation of power from a centralized, hub-spoke perspective, questions were asked about how, at the level of the local, it might be possible to generate electricity that did not depend on the hub-spoke grid? What if a different kind of question were asked that would bring together people in local contexts with skilled experts in a variety of fields to find alternative solutions to energy production? In the context of this question, a new set of words started to appear and provide promise, words such as *nodal*, *clustering*, *linking*, *distributive* and *multipolar*. This imagination started to slowly reshape the thinking of leaders toward what would become a revolutionary approach to the question of electric production and distribution. Like the application of wheels to suitcases, it did not involve the wholesale deconstruction of existing structures but, as strange as it may sound, the application of small-scale technologies to what was already happening at the local and everyday. Within this shift in perspective lies a dawning recognition that the answers to the challenges being faced did not lie primarily at the center of a hub but in the ways thousands of people in local, everyday situations were learning to experiment in the midst of disruptive change. The revolution, so to speak, started from below and in the ordinary. It did not begin or call for the dismantling or wholesale change of existing structures but the willingness to make seemingly small experiments at the local level.

This kind of imaginative shift is what is being proposed as the way in which the denominations might discern how they can change their organizational cultures.

This changed imagination started happening in Denmark around the midpoint of the first decade of this millennium. People wrestling with the question of electrical energy started seeing the situation with different lenses. They began in a simple way, with a different kind of question: What if they started with the assumption that there were already thousands of electrical cars spread all over Denmark connected and plugged into homes that were themselves smart in terms of electrical needs? What would happen if homes and cars, instead of being dependent on a traditional generating plant hundreds of miles away, were connected locally to a series of wind turbines and ancillary sun voltage cells? What if homes were designed in such a way that they became generators of electricity? Interestingly, the design of these homes became a work of adaptive learning.[4] Alongside these innovations, what if smart meters which read power needs in a home correlated those needs with local power supplies connecting both homes and the local power grids to determine when to turn on and off things like washing machines, dishwashers and plugged-in electric cars?

These "what ifs" are already becoming the practical reality in Denmark (also in Germany; it is spreading to Spain and Italy, tentatively moving into the United Kingdom and coming to a town in your area soon). In brief, the fundamental hub-spoke default that dominated planning imagination for over a century is being decentered as another way of seeing the world (metaphor) come into focus. In this other imagination, answers are found in the thousands of small ways locales and skilled professionals interconnect to other locales and professionals across diverse geography to engage and resolve the disruptive, adaptive challenges that lie before so many organizational systems formed in the twentieth century.

Organizational systems must now learn a whole different way of functioning. They are required to develop a new imagination that reframes their structural relationships in such a way that this kind of partnership between and across the local becomes the primary generator of learning. This new context invites denominational systems to see their role in terms of cultivating environments, spaces, means and opportunities for connectivity and distributive learning alongside the local contexts in their whole system.

SHAPING AN ALTERNATIVE ORGANIZATIONAL FUTURE

We are standing at the front end of the emergence of a significantly different imagination for organizational functionality. It will open a profoundly different world of opportunity, moving us beyond twentieth-century defaults for organizational change. The basic metaphors informing this imagination, using electrical generation as an illustration, are *local*, *distributive*, *networked* and *smart grid*. The term *smart grid*, for example, refers to a confluence of technologies to provide a means of assessing, monitoring and intelligently responding to the behaviors of electric power users connected in local areas in order to efficiently distribute reliable, economic and sustainable electrical services (see fig. 9.1). This, however, is only the beginning point in a much broader revolution wherein smart grid technology gets linked with an expansive network of locally based communities that become, themselves, the basic units of distribution and generation. Note that the creative space in this adaptive work is the interactive learning communities that are created in the local and in relationship with skilled experts in a wide variety of disciplines.

The distributive is being built around this interrelationality. It is also about numerous "locals" in communication with one another as smart, interconnected learning communities.

The possibility that is emerging is for denominations to remake themselves in the form of a distributed network in relationship with multiple local contexts generating experiments and responses to the challenges of mission and ministry at this time. This doesn't require these denominations to start with major organizational or structural change. Rather, much as in the Danish and German examples, begin with small experiments working with numbers of learning communities across the country.

Figure 9.1. Distributive systems

The cultivation and resourcing of interconnected, localized networks determining their own challenges, actions and responses to the shifting changes of their environments should become the primary focus and work of denominational structures as well as their staffs. This shift in locus, energy and attention is not a simple challenge. It involves a difficult transitional process of culture change. This is part of the shift in social imaginaries that will need to be embraced if the denominations are to discover a meaningful future in the midst of the massive changes reshaping the West.

The exciting thing about these proposals is that already, across denominational systems and among congregations, in all kinds of off-stage ways that can't be immediately measured or quantified, people in differing local contexts are becoming the incubators of a new imagination with their own tentative experiments in the local.[5] Therefore, under the surface of the frenetic work of denominational leaders at national and regional levels, other things begin to happen. While some localities reactively dig in, demanding a return to established practices, others simply ignore what national and regional bodies are doing and start experimenting. For increasing numbers of people national and regional bodies are more and more irrelevant to what is at stake in the local. There is little energy or credibility left for one more national or regional project everyone is to join. People in local contexts are going their own way.

Alternative imaginations are incubating across diffuse, nonorganized groups (they will often tell you they don't know what they're doing or that what they are up to is of no account) across a multitude of localities. In the midst of these quiet stirrings are the intimations, the tender, fragile shoots of what the Spirit is continually calling forth in our midst. Usually, such experimenting isn't organized. It is largely the result of a restless testing and trying out of things by people disillusioned with existing responses to crisis. But make no mistake, it is also precisely the ways in which the Holy Spirit goes about new creation (2 Cor 5:17). These are the gestations and birth pangs of God's counterintuitive future for the churches. It is already happening across all types and styles of churches. As Sparks, Soerens and Friesen indicate, there is already a plethora of such experiments going on for those with eyes to see. It is easy to discount many of these experiments because some will look silly from inside current defaults. Others simply fail, and yet others are carried out by people who, demonstrably, don't know what they're doing. There is plenty of room for criticism and endless illustrations of their improbability, which is the case when people are, well, experimenting. As some experiments get traction, however, by connecting with what is happening in their local contexts,[6] something else emerges—a sense among diverse groups in many differing localities that there is a different way of being church, a different way of working.

This has already started. Something is afoot; the genie is out of the bottle and it won't be put back in by any policies or procedures.[7] As this shift unfolds (it can't be managed or timelined), the ways existing denominational structures are currently functioning out of the defaults outlined earlier will rapidly become irrelevant for the majority who once saw them as an indispensable part of their world. We have already entered this period. We are not just passing through the unraveling of denominational life, but if these denominations can grasp how the Spirit is already out ahead in so many places, then they can be remade.

We are not living in a postdenominational era but at the end of the time that shaped their identities and roles through the twentieth century. The Eurotribal denominations have an amazing potential before them in terms of their future. As an Anglican, the theological traditions within these denominations offers a rich space to reimagine the ways of being God's people at this time. We are entering yet another phase of denominational life where denominations will need to ask how they might appropriately adapt to the contexts of ministry in which their congregations find themselves.[8] In the distributive age a primary capacity is the empowering of the people of God, in local contexts, to discern (through experimentation) their own actions for addressing the challenges of mission. The denominations can play a critical role in this diffused, distributive environment. This new phase of denominational life is about cultivating spaces for forming distributive learning communities that collectively discern through experimentation the shape of mission in their shifting contexts and communicate this learning with one another other across localities.

Finally, but by no means least, there is an opportunity here for national, regional and local leaders to reclaim the imagination and vocation that should be at the core of their work—the role of theologians of the ordinary and everyday.[9] The great need in this ending of one denominational phase and the emergence of the distributive is for leaders with the capacities to function as theologians of the everyday at several levels. First, they must learn how to practically reenter and reframe the tradition of their denomination in terms of the new space the Spirit has brought us to. This is an urgent missiological need for the Eurotribal denominations for whom the stories of power, place and dominance around some theological frames and tribal customs from sixteenth-century Europe have little relevance to this turning moment. These kinds of local theologians, like detectives of divinity, know their own stories and traditions at very deep levels. They live into those traditions, not out of nostalgia but a conviction that within their founding stories lie important clues to the directions in which the disruptive Spirit is leading their tribe.

Anglicans might, for example, rediscover that the *parish* was, in its initial engagements in post-Roman England, a secular term taken up as a profoundly missiological engagement with a society that was disintegrating. They might see again that bishops are the shapers of missional communities in the midst of societies falling apart. Baptists might rediscover that their founding identity was not rooted in so-called Baptist theological distinctives (these theological claims came later as a way of rationalizing and legitimating what had occurred),[10] but in an intuitive gifting of the Spirit that kept gnawing at them with the sense that the churches had lost touch with the peoples of their culture. Therefore, they risked their lives to become a courageous people willing to test and experiment for the sake of the kingdom. In their denominational forms Baptists have lost many aspects of this basic DNA of disruption, dis-ease and the willingness to risk in the unknown.

Second, in the language of Clemens Sedmak, the denominations at national, middle and local levels need theologians who are "artisans of a new humanity," forming congregations out of the materials, resources, colors, tastes and smells of the local.[11] What is starting to emerge (the Parish Collective is an early signifier, one of the green shoots so suggestive of a massive stirring happening just under the surface but still out of sight) are multiple, interacting networks that are wrestling with ways to address intersecting challenges of being God's people in their contexts. Denominational systems have the opportunity to learn how they might interact and partner with these contexts across their own systems. These are the new spaces from which imaginative actions emerge.

In this new context national and regional organizational systems are being decentered from the customary roles they have played. They can have a vital role in the new space, but it is profoundly different. Rather than being the places of expertise and centered-set priorities, they become conduits for generating environments for local engagements to flourish and interconnect with other localities in learning communities. They become more like cultivators of interrelated networks working off one another rather than a centrally guided system of experts.

This is the kind of shift in imagination, role, identity, power and functionality denominational structures and their leaders must embrace. Existing forms of denominational structure are becoming irrelevant. This does not mean the end but rather the transition of denominations into yet another phase. An emerging distributive culture rooted in the local and everyday offers to denominational systems a Spirit-framed invitation to reimagine themselves for mission. If old-fashioned electrical companies, birthed by a hub-spoke mentality, can make this shift, surely those given leadership among God's people can do the same.

From Here to There

Who, then, were the real city builders? Planners and urban designers obviously had a role to play, but so did city engineers, politicians, mall owners, business people and local communities acting individually and together in implementing changes. Formal plans aside, the real outcomes at street level arose from the cumulative effect of many seemingly unrelated actions by many parties. And many of the key decisions were made by unseen hands both distant and local, which were not necessarily conscious that they were reshaping the city.

Ken Greenberg, *Walking Home*

INTRODUCTION

What is involved in a denomination entering into this level of imaginative change? This chapter offers proposals for addressing existing defaults and discerning a way forward that does not require the endless, tiring restructuring that has characterized North American churches for the past fifty or more years. Metaphors such as *distributive, emergence, grafting* and *cultivating* are replacing those of *centered, restructuring* and *reengineering*. Processes of experimentation and adaptation are beginning to replace those of strategic planning.[1] The critical role of local networks is starting to replace that of center-shaped management. The new metaphors are about imagination rather than hitting the bull's-eye, about risk rather than health, about seeing God in the neighborhood rather than national programs for discipleship.

This rich change in language suggests that part of the critical work of denominational leaders at national and regional levels involves becoming aware of language, its use and the way metaphors play such a significant role in shaping, reinforcing and transforming defaults. For a long time the trend has been to take our language usage for granted, as if it conveyed precisely what everyone understood and assumed. Moving in and out of multiple denominational systems indicates that over the decades each has built up a whole language house that is used to signal what behavior is appropriate, how people are to act inside a group and what it means to believe inside that group. Over a long period of time certain kinds of metaphors came into usage as if everyone knew what they meant. Thus words like *discipleship, spirituality* and *evangelism* became shorthand for the way a people within a system (Baptists or Reformed or Anglican) were to believe and act. Denominational structures and leaders then simply created programs and events that reinforced the taken-for-granted assumptions buried in these language games. As denominations are propelled into yet another phase of life, it becomes more and more incumbent for their leaders to learn how to attend to language, and how it is shaping the imagination and default actions of themselves and the people in their system. This attention to language and metaphor will assist leaders to understand why one of their important tasks is to change the language games of their systems.

THE LANGUAGE OF LEADERSHIP

An example of this comes from the ways the language of "clergy leadership" operates in these systems.[2] In a workshop involving a group of Baptist leaders (clergy and nonclergy), people were instructed to form groups of five to work on a set of questions. Part of the instructions asked clergy to refrain from speaking too much or taking the lead in the discussions. As the groups dug into their assignment, it became clear that clergy were doing the bulk of the talking as well as providing primary guidance within their groups. This was not just a function of overzealous (or hard of hearing) clergy. It also illustrated the presence of a powerful default—

namely, the ways in which generations of people in congregations have been socialized to defer to clergy in these kinds of discussions. The fascinating element about this workshop experience was that the group was composed of Baptists, who are by nature very independent and don't like being told what to do by anyone. But there it was, even among Baptists, this strange game in which the language of "clergy" ipso facto causes even highly individualized people to defer. The interesting thing was that not even the clergy were aware of this going on until it was pointed out to them. Both clergy and nonordained leaders were equally implicated in a language game that gave preference to the authority of the ordained. Being aware of how language games are at work shaping the defaults of a community has now become a critical, basic skill for leaders in the midst of disruptive change.

Furthermore, the language of "leadership" conveys a language game in which both clergy and people assume that the responsibility of the clergy person, as leader, is to develop solutions to fix a problem or effectively grow a healthy church. The results are predictable. Some leaders, feeling the weight of this burden, are overwhelmed with its impossible demands; others succumb to the expectations resident in the language by becoming top-down CEOs of their church corporation. In each case, what is maintained is the default belief that clergy (church professionals, church executives) have the answers.

The epigraph at the beginning of this chapter by the architect Ken Greenberg illustrates why this language game is (1) an illusion, and (2) blinds us to how organizational systems actually engage hard situations. After more than forty years of experience in designing and reimagining forms of city life, Greenberg is well aware that the notions of leadership described earlier are silly, false and misleading. In retrospect what creates a great city is not primarily the leadership of professionals and experts (even though they have important roles), nor is it all the formal planning these groups propose. The real sources of transformation are the myriad of ordinary people working at street level, on the ground, out of their intuitions and interactions. It is the cumulative effect of all these seemingly unrelated interactions that reshape a city (and will reinvent the denominations for this new time). Greenberg is describing the distributive era as it was emerging in the early 1970s in the field of urban planning (specifically Jane Jacobs and the imaginative new movement of city development she birthed).[3] Again, we need to develop an awareness of how our language of "leadership," "expert," "professional" and "executive" actually reinforces defaults like those mentioned earlier.

THE CHALLENGE OF TRUST

Across denominational systems right now, trust is in very short supply.[4] The imaginative change required to create the levels of innovation outlined in the previous chapters requires a readiness, across a denominational system, to trust again. This is a daunting task. The challenge of trust operates at two levels. First, the depths of mistrust that currently exist across every level of denominational life are significant. There are multiple reasons for this mistrust. It has developed over several generations as denominational systems, seeking to address the cascading implosion of their narratives, began to turn on each other in blame games. It is a normal, human trait for a social group in crisis to turn on and cannibalize one another. As the viability of the corporate denomination eroded late in the twentieth century, national and regional leaders responded with restructuring programs and personnel cuts. A predictable outcome was the move of program offices, national groups and midlevel judicatories into self-protective silos. The subsystems then entered the blame game, each viewing the other as a threat to be managed and a problem to be solved in a win-lose game of dwindling resources and lowered expectations. The results were that within national bodies and across national-regional systems, people communicated less and less with one another, or the communication was functional rather than strategic. The overall result was the increasing dysfunction of the denomination at all levels. Like continental shelves, national, regional and local clashed into one another in a devolving blame game.

These patterns are now sedimented into the default responses of these groups toward one another. Working with national and regional elements of denominations, this story is told over and over again. Sitting among national executives of denominations I hear the same, familiar story (no matter what the denomination) of how "they" (referring to regional or local leadership) demonstrate no appreciation for the work of national, regional or local leadership under difficult times. These same national, regional or local leaders complain about the ways leadership in the other areas want to control access to money or congregations without reference to the legitimate roles of each other's organizational claims. This blame-game liturgy is present at all levels of the system. It has now become a default, an automatic response mechanism dominating the relationships within and across denominational systems, demonizing the other inside one's own tribe.

Addressing this crisis of trust is one of the most pressing challenges the denominations have to face if there is to be a fundamental change of imagination. This endless, repetitive, default iteration of mistrust, accusation and finger pointing is the current norm. There are more than enough stories in the arsenals of leaders across these systems to justify the culture of blame and mistrust that exists. The problem is that at this moment denominations can ill afford this tragic reactivity. What is needed is a change in mind (Rom 12:1-2). All the elements of a massive tsunami of change are boiling just beneath the surface. There is little space left for the denominations, as they are currently configured, to play the current blame game with one another. Even though denominations are not going away, existing leadership has little time left within existing cultural narratives to make a difference. There are significant legacy issues at stake here! The current imagination shaping the denominations and outlined in the earlier sections of this book will disappear very quickly. The question is whether these leaders want to be a part of creating the context for a different future.

If the culture of blame and counterblame, of accusation and counteraccusation, of us-them, of story after story of how the other has been in the wrong would have produced anything other than a downward spiral of destructive acrimony, it would have manifested itself by now. No single group across a denomination has ownership or clarity on how to address this reality, but it has to be faced. Rehearsing the other's failures and one's own list of grievances may release tension for a time. It may create one's own internal coterie of like-minded people; it may provide one with some semblance of self-justification, but it won't get at what's at stake. A readiness to risk acting in trust with one another is essential to creating a resilience that releases adaptive imagination.

If the first challenge is the depth of mistrust across every level of denominational leadership, the second is that this crisis of trust goes deeper than specific people who are actors in denominational structures. It is also about a pervasive kind of unraveling that affects not just the churches but practically every level of civil society. The case can be made that one of the more positive characteristics of the corporate denomination in the twentieth century was that it, like other elements of civil society, brought people together around a common sense of story and purpose. This is what might be called the public good. Leaders at national, regional and local levels saw themselves joined together in the belief that this denominational story in which their lives and often the histories of their families were involved brought them together inside something that was important not just for themselves but the public good of the society. What has happened over the past third of a century is that this sense of calling into a beloved community existing for the sake of commitments beyond pressure groups or identity issues has evaporated. Adam Seligman writes about the "perceived and growing difficulty in maintaining the very principle of Public Good in contemporary politics and the sense of commitment and responsibility to the Public Good that must, of necessity, go with it. We are increasingly . . . but shareholders rather than stakeholders in the myriad ventures in our life-world."[5]

We are indeed increasingly shareholders with personal rights that need to be met rather than stakeholders in something bigger than ourselves. There has been a huge, tragic erosion of a basic trust directed toward the common good that once formed a critical part of the common narrative across North American societies. The loss of this kind of trust is mirrored in the denominations where increasing levels of internal fracturing result in people splitting apart into single-issue pressure groups. What was once taken to be difference that was lived with together for the sake of a larger vision is now the basis for division. In these divisions the issues are not primarily theological (as the claims declare) but the ways the denominations have become implicated in this broader dissolution of a common narrative for a greater end. We are witnessing, and implicated in, the pushing of associational life and social contract to their radical ends, wherein specific, often personal, issues are the basis for fragmentation.

In some denominations the only elements really keeping them together are pension plans and property rights. Neither is an expression of people seeking together to live by a narrative bigger than themselves; rather, they symbolize a radical extension of self-expression and social contract. The current inability of denominations to weather these waters has more to do with the ways their leaders are implicated in prevalent narratives of power, control, management and mistrust. This dissipation of common commitment to a bigger story has produced a widespread disillusionment with existing structures and processes within the denominations. The loss of trust in the denominations and their abilities to address the challenges faced by the churches makes many of the current discussions in these systems about change and renewal empty exercises. On the ground, in the congregations and among local clergy there is little expectation or confidence at this moment that the denominations have any role to play in addressing the crisis of the churches. That being said, there is yet space for the denominations to invite their churches on a journey that will change this situation. They have an important role to play in reframing a narrative of being a people together for something bigger than themselves. This remains a live promise of the Spirit.

This assessment is not a whimsical nostalgia or a naive, romantic wish. It is founded on the conviction that God is the primary active agent in the midst of all this unraveling of church and society. It is funded by the conviction that the Spirit has not finished with the denominations but has for them a calling, a vocation, in the midst of these strange new spaces. Jesus did, indeed, call men and women to discipleship, to the risk of giving their lives for something bigger than themselves. Yet any honest reading of the New Testament tells us that these disciples who changed the world were not the best and brightest; they were not the gurus or A-type early adopters. They were mostly ordinary men and women, plodders who couldn't clearly figure out what was going on, who spent more time catching up with the Spirit than defining what God was doing. They hardly qualify as experts.

Amid all the claims about the end of denominations and congregations, this gives me reason to trust that God has not changed—the future will emerge, as it always has, from these old wine skins most folk are ready to throw away for the new wine of their imagination.[6] Can we trust this God who continually messes with almost all our categories of what God is doing, what the church is to be about and how denominations are to function to bring forth that which cannot be predicted, strategized or schemed? The question is whether or not denominational leaders will choose to trust this reality of God's agency in ways that cause them to lay down the blame game and turn away from the growing commitment to associational defaults shaped by single issues. A first step for denominational leaders is to create spaces of trust across their system.

Creating spaces of trust: Beginning with ourselves. First, it must begin with denominational leaders themselves choosing to act differently in terms of their relationships within the system! In Luke 10:1-12, Jesus provides the Seventy with a set of instructions (disciplines) for traveling on the way.[7] Two practices shed light on the work of trust that denominational leaders need to cultivate. First, they are instructed to go without baggage (no extra shoes, cloak, etc.; they are dependent on the other, not protected, self-contained and insulated). This means deciding to lay down one's list of "facts" about the "others" around the denominational tables. This is a fundamental act of spiritual discipline, a choice to believe that as the primary agent God is present among a group of co-leaders who have become antagonists and strangers to one another. If denominational leaders have not created and given this space to one another in their own shops, they will never do this across their systems.

Second, the text invites the Seventy to speak "shalom" into the lives of the others in one's village. This is also a spiritual practice of transformation based in the trust that the Spirit of God is present in the spaces where shalom is spoken. This is a practice that invites denominational leaders to create environments in which they are first, before all else, speaking shalom to the others at the table. These practices are critical initiating points for creating new spaces of trust inside denominational systems. They concretize the conviction that God has no space for the destructive drives that turn "them" into the other, the scapegoats of our own anxieties.

In one national denominational office the level of discourse between different sections of the organization had descended to a place of massive distrust and accusation. This was seen in the siloed world in which each section lived apart from the other. Heads of these sections met monthly, but it was plain that they only went through the pro-forma motions of filling the required time for the meeting. Outside of these meetings there was hardly any communication. The list of wrongs that each had created of the other was long and growing. There was no trust in the room, even while the denomination as a whole was coming apart and respect for national offices dissolving. When the group was presented with this reality in one of their regular meetings, there was no disagreement, but the silence also said that no one knew what to do to break the nexus of blame, retreat, accusation and deepening mistrust. Individually, they were good people; they longed to experience again the reality of God's life in the midst of their denomination. They had worked hard over many years to serve the church for the sake of the gospel, but this nexus of system fragmentation, co-blaming and retreat from one another had become a default that felt intractable. How could they unravel the tangled knot of accusation and mistrust that always sat in the middle of the room whenever they met? They knew that across the denomination in all of the regions, a lot of midlevel judicatory leaders and local clergy knew this was the case. They all knew that they stared at one another across a rapidly eroding denomination. What was to be done?

Instead of trying to mediate all the felt (real and assumed) accusations and hurts, these leaders could choose a different course of action. What if they chose to leave their baggage behind? What if they chose to act as if they trusted one another in order to focus on a common direction for the sake of the denominational household God had called them to oversee? What if they came together around a common journey to address the realities of church they no longer knew how to manage or control? This group of leaders chose to take this journey. It would be a journey into which they wanted to invite other leaders at the middle and local levels. It wouldn't be a big, new strategic plan for revitalization.

Rather, it would be a journey shaped around a specific question that applied to national, midlevel and local: *What are the challenges we currently face for which we presently have no answer but must address if we're to live into God's future for us?*

When these national executives first shared this journey with other leaders across the denomination, all the existing mistrust immediately rose to the surface. (Let's be clear: there are still those in the system who continue to live inside this default of mistrust and blame, and not everyone was willing to get on board.) These national leaders were accused of one more top-down action and blamed for not consulting with others (even though that was precisely what they were doing in numerous gatherings and meetings). But then something else began to happen. At the middle and local levels, people began to see a change. They saw that these national leaders were acting differently; they were trusting and taking risks with one another. Others began to sense that while their proposal for this journey might not be perfect, it was a genuine invitation, and these national leaders were not in control of its directions or outcomes. As midlevel and local leaders began to see this change at the national level, the environment across the denomination began to change. Trust was growing; a fragile bridge was being built across which people who had refused to engage with one another could walk in a common journey of discovering how the Spirit might be shaping a new imagination in their midst. It began with a small number of key leaders choosing to act as if they did trust one another.

Creating spaces of trust: Experiments, not megaprojects. As discussed in part one, a key reason for denominational failure is that practically all the things that made them successful for most of the twentieth century are now the cause of their failure. One of the most helpful exercises we have used in getting at this reality is a multiple-day retreat in which, among other things, leaders list all the initiatives in their system over the last twenty years. That grows to become quite a long list. We then work with them to identify the reasons for those initiatives and create spaces where they can honestly assess their effects. Most of the time these lists of initiatives are based on the DNA that had made denominations successful in the twentieth century. These leaders recognize this and, at the same time, also realize that these remain the primary frames and skills they are operating out of. This realization is important in order to frame the journey of trust they will need to develop. It takes time and is not achieved in a few meetings or retreats.

The upshot of this process is for denominational leaders to recognize that they actually don't know, therefore, what to do. This is not a criticism of these leaders. Few, in practically every area of life and work at this moment, have a clear idea about how to proceed in this new space. The challenges of this critical turning point, however, must be named and addressed. One such challenge is how to name honestly that we are at the end of our given abilities when we live inside a culture of deep mistrust. It is extremely difficult, if not impossible, for leaders to own the fact that they no longer know what to do and that the existing patterns of their leadership are ineffective. Furthermore, another challenge is that precisely because of this mistrust, with its concomitant culture of blame and siloing, these leaders will find themselves actually working harder within their existent DNA even while using new language to describe their practices. The evidence of this is when national organizations launch one more major program in areas such as discipleship, evangelism or congregational revitalization. Each is an indication of this underlying DNA reasserting itself in a culture of mistrust and fear.

Part of the problem here is that once these leaders realize they're facing challenges for which they have no answers but which must be addressed if the system is to thrive, everything feels like a leap into the unknown. Such leaps are not easily embraced. At this point it becomes clear that denominational transformation is not a matter of one more program or turning clergy into CEOs of growth models. National and midlevel leaders become aware they are facing challenges they've never met before but have little to no sense of how to engage these challenges. The most dangerous thing to do at this juncture is create some major program. Yet this is exactly what leaders feel they must do! They feel the imperative to act, to lead, to give direction. Yielding to these fight-or-flight instincts is unhelpful. Fragile trust needs to be protected and strengthened at this juncture. The way to do this is to resist the big programmatic solution

(the new generating plant for the energy-starved electrical company) and
create space for experiments in co-learning across the system.

EXPERIMENTS, RESILIENCE, ADAPTATION

Experiments. When the notion of a distributive electrical grid formed out
of a network of specifically designed houses and a reversed imagination
for the place and direction of electrical generation was initially proposed,
it was greeted with a wealth of skepticism. Before it could grip people's
imagination, some small experiments had to be developed that showed
people there was a different way of creating energy in the northern parts
of Europe. When Jane Jacobs came onto the scene in the 1950s and
1960s, modernism in architecture and city building was at its zenith.
Huge towers housing people and massive highways transporting them to
work, play and shopping at newly minted suburban malls were the or-
thodoxy of the day around which city councils created urban plans and
made bylaws. Her notions of the livable city sounded out of step with
what experts and professionals "knew" was needed for people to thrive
in the modern, urban world. When Jacobs moved to Toronto in 1968,
after her battles in New York with the iconic Robert Moses, she caught
the imagination of a small group of young city councilors (David Crombie
and John Sewell) who sensed something was massively amiss about all
the "urban renewal" that was bulldozing old neighborhoods and replacing them with towers that warehoused people and removed them
from the grounded connectivity of the local neighborhood.[8]

Crombie and Sewell, together with architects and urban planners such
as Ken Greenberg, had instincts and hunches, but they were unformed,
and no one knew what alternative ways for forming urban life might look
like. Their criticisms and assaults on the dominant planning models were
wonderful theater, but for almost everyone else on city council or in
planning groups it was idealism uprooted from reality. Only as people
like Crombie, Sewell and Jacobs found small places over time in which
to experiment did things start to slowly change. The experiments,
whether in electrical generation or city development, became the impetus for cultural transformations that no megaproject or top-down
program could achieve. There are important reasons for this.

Experiments give systems the opportunity to become learning communities in the fragile spaces where trust needs to be rebuilt across segments of a social group. Given the drawn-out traumas of denominational life over the past quarter century, few are ready to believe or engage in one more round of someone else's plan. Each time a denominational group draws up a plan to revitalize churches or roll out a new design for discipleship, the common response is some form of "here we go again," "been there–done that" and "it won't make any difference." Experiments provide the context for a different kind of table around which people can connect and try things. However, this only works if they are designed to be genuine learning communities seeking to explore together the adaptive challenges commonly owned by everyone involved. The distributive age means experiments emerge from attending to the local and being on the ground among the ordinary and everyday.

Such experiments create environments of learning that don't presume there are experts and laity in unequal relationship with one another. Experiments are about how a group of people who come with different assumptions and attitudes enter a liminal situation. They have finally recognized that while there are still differing gifts and capacities around the table, no one is any longer an expert with the solutions. In this space of becoming and community of learning, they test ways of developing practices for engaging the challenges before them, but this is done in ways in which all are learners and all are teachers. These are critical elements in rebuilding the kind of trust needed to form the environment within an organizational structure that can lead to new imagination.

In this sense, the language of "experimentation" provides the spaces for everyone—national, midlevel and local—to honestly own the fact that within the context of the experiment they are all genuinely learners and not experts; therefore, no one is in control. Liminal spaces require the ending of the power games (usually fought over turf, money and control), which remain prevalent across the denominations. Within this narrative of experimenting leaders find the safe spaces to test out new habits, attitudes and practices in forming local missional life. They can actually work at something they haven't done before and, by definition, don't know how to do. This context of experimentation creates the table for leaders across a denominational system to address the question, *What are the challenges we currently face for which we presently have no answer but must address if we're to live into God's future for us?*

Two very clear adaptive challenges lie at the heart of denominational systems that have to be approached from the perspective of experimentation: (1) overcoming the hub-spoke default to embrace the new, distributive age of denominational life, and (2) building communities of trust in order to form experiments among a liminal people. The primary locus of these experiments needs to be the local.[9] That means congregations in their contexts of neighborhood, work and play are the primary locus of experimentation. The reasons for this have already been discussed. To recap: first, it is among God's people in ordinary, everyday life in neighborhoods that the Spirit is already gestating all the intimations of God's future; and, second, in this space it will be distributive networks of local experiments that begin to show forth the contours of what it will mean to be church.

This means the primary role of national and midlevel denominational systems is to create the environments and spaces for these experiments and distributive networks of learning to emerge. Questions about the organizational and structural roles of these denominational leaders cannot be answered in the abstract or by returning to definitions of current practice. Only by implicating themselves in becoming part of the learning experiments at these local, distributive levels will denominational leaders and their boards be able to answer the questions, *What then is our role? What kinds of skills and capacities do we need to enable effective mission-shaped denominational life?*

These questions can't be answered at the front end of this journey or codified into abstract proposals based on current readings of biblical passages or the written forms (confessions, books of order/discipline, restructuring proposals) of denominational systems. Each of these sources (the Bible, traditions and organizational structures) have been colonized by existent legitimating narratives and socialized by forms of leadership that use long-established, common forms of language (bishop, pastor, elder, cleric, etc.) but in fact have been reinterpreted in terms of functionality and actual practice through the denominational defaults of the past century.

In this way denominational leaders cannot stand outside the need for experimenting as if their roles were inviolable because of some esoteric, romantic notions of biblical identity or traditions handed down. These leaders must understand that they are themselves deeply implicated in this risky business of creating experiments to engage missional challenges in the local. Their role can no longer be that of the professional or ordained managing a process while they are in fact circumscribed by this role from being changed. The question of the role and identity of mid-level and national denominational leaders can only be addressed as they become implicated in the experiments and as they learn to assess their roles through the rearview mirror.

The kinds of experiments required are like those of the electrical companies or the new movements in city planning. They are about learning how to create distributed networks of local communities, congregations and parishes that are, through their interconnections, learning together how to be the generators of God's future in their contexts. The experiments become learning laboratories in which local, national and midlevel people enter liminal space together as they seek the ways in which each become midwives, poets and gardeners in discovering the shapes of God's future. This kind of description suggests the kind of journey denominations need to embark on and the kinds of learning all their leaders need to enter. It is not an easy journey; it calls for critical new learning and the testing of capacities not immediately natural or native to leaders.

Resilience. I was recently driving my ten-year-old Mercedes along the main street of our town and began to have a disconcerting feeling about the car. For the first time it felt like the car was continually going "thump, thump, thump" over every little bump in the road. Instead of riding smoothly over the road as it had done all along, it was feeling like the whole car was being hit by every dip in the road and had lost the capacity to absorb the bumps along the way. The mechanic looked at the old car and told me the front ball joints needed replacing. The job of the ball joints is to absorb shocks to the car so that, along with the shock absorbers, the car can run smoothly across the roads. This ability to absorb the bumps is an example of resilience. It is the capacity of an organism or organization to absorb shocks from ever-changing environments by anticipating and tolerating disruption without losing basic functionalities. This is not the current status of denominations. Indeed, it seems that now every small shock or bump is felt like a huge hit— there has been a massive loss of resilience. Across a number of large denominations there exists a built-in fear that the next disagreement, no matter how small, will tip the whole system into disruptions it can no longer manage.

There is something about resilience that's counterintuitive. The more established and efficient a system has become over time (as, for example, the car industry in North America in the first two-thirds of the twentieth century) the more its resilience weakens. The more a system organizes and structures its life to function effectively within a specific environment (the establishment of taken-for-granted defaults) the less capable it becomes to deal with major disruptions when its environment changes. It loses the capacity to bounce back.

In Van Gelder's metaphor of denominational DNA, the more effective denominations were at developing a strong DNA, defining and shaping their systems, structures and roles, the less resilient they are in this place of massive cultural transformation. When a well-established system faces disruptive change, its DNA causes it to quickly apply existing skills and solutions. When these tactics fail (e.g., restructuring or programs of discipleship training), blame and accusation go up across a system. The result is that people hurt one another and trust plummets. This default cycle of DNA, existing tactics and mutual blame is self-destructive to the system. This is where the framing of change in terms of experiments becomes absolutely necessary for the denomination. This kind of experimentation calls for adaptive work. This means addressing our key question: *What are the challenges we currently face for which we presently have no answer but must address if we're to live into God's future for us?*

Adaptation. Adaptation is the capacity of an organization to change basic defaults in order to thrive. To change, the organization as a whole (not just pockets here and there) must become adaptive-driven.

This involves a decentered process focused on distributed networks of local people forming learning communities wherein the people who actually live in these local contexts are working on adaptive challenges *they* are naming rather than those determined by experts and professionals. Resilience and adaptation are the work of the people. It is within this context that national, midlevel and local clergy must reimagine their roles.

The language of "adaptation" has entered the common parlance of church systems much as the language of "missional" did a dozen years ago. Adaptive language is helpful, but some important cautions are in order. One of the ongoing defaults of church systems is to adopt language that has entered the common practice of the culture and use it with little or no reflection as a new technique. In the late 1990s *missional* entered the vocabulary as a way of understanding that mission (missio Dei) isn't just something the church does alongside many other functionalities but is what the church is in its essence.[10] In the space of little more than a decade, however, that word entered the common narrative of the church and was quickly turned back into a series of techniques for church health, growth and effectiveness. In other words, the defaults remain so powerful that it is in the nature of the churches to turn helpful frames back into techniques that enable them to manage (not change) their situations within existing imaginations. This is already happening with the language of "adaptive work."

The other caution is about what happens when a new method or technique enters the language game of a church system. This book has argued that the disruption facing the churches is about God's agency and especially the disruptive work of the Spirit pushing the Eurotribal churches into spaces they cannot manage or control. If this basic theological and ecclesiological perspective is lost or dislodged as the primary lens of our situation, then other language games take precedence. In so doing, *adaptive* becomes yet one more technique for managing inside our defaults. With these two cautions in place, it is helpful to provide a brief summary of what's involved in the idea of adaptive work.

Ronald Heifetz and Marty Linsky popularized the idea of adaptive change and explored why this kind of change does not fit with the usual authority of experts and professionals. In describing adaptive change as the work of the people they suggest that a different organizational and leadership imagination is required.[11] Heifetz and Linsky identify two types of challenges: *adaptive* and *technical*. Each kind of challenge requires a different kind of approach. Whether an organization faces a technical or adaptive challenge determines the type of leadership authority required. Technical challenges refer to those which can be remedied using existing skills and within existing organizational structures. Examples of this would be setting up a new accounting system, wiring an organization for high-speed Internet, planning a national gathering, organizing the schedule for an event, preparing a teaching or preaching session, developing a workshop on evangelism or discipleship, and the like. When a clergy person plans a marriage, funeral or liturgy, he or she leads out of existing expertise and within well-understood roles. Such activities, for the professional, don't require new learning or the organizational structure to behave in a different manner. They are amenable to current know-how, expertise and experience. The habits, attitudes, practices and imagination of the leader do not have to change—they remain the same after the action.

Other challenges, such as how to engage a changed, multicultural, secularized community when congregations are monocultural, or how to develop effective discipleship in a radically consumerist society, can't be addressed by experts or within the existing organizational structures. An adaptive challenge requires more than setting new priorities or developing new programs. It demands a basic change in the hearts, minds, attitudes and habits of the people involved. The focus of the adaptive work is not the skills and expertise of leaders, but on the work of the people. A leader's job is to invite the people into adaptive work (which we often don't want to face because it involves loss). Leaders thus work like midwives creating environments in which people can give birth to locally owned responses to challenges they identify out of their own engagements. Heifetz and Linsky suggest several important distinctions between technical and adaptive work (see table 9.1).

Table 9.1. Distinctions Between Technical and Adaptive Work

Technical	Adaptive
Clear goals	Murky future
Known methods/expertise	New learning
Current resources	Unidentified resources
Familiar roles and abilities—work out of authority	Unfamiliar roles and abilities—work of the people
Manageable change	Unpredictable change

Tables like Heifetz and Linsky's, showing neat differentiations between the two types, don't quite communicate the reality on the ground. What makes this process difficult for organizations and their leaders is that an organization continues to face ongoing technical challenges it must address day in and day out within existing expertise and structures at the same time as it must confront adaptive challenges that can't be addressed in this way. The left side of the table doesn't disappear. Technical challenges continue. Indeed, in organizations facing major adaptive challenges the need for technical work increases as concerns and anxieties across the organization increase. It is difficult for leaders to know when their management, expertise and organizational defaults might be driving their well-crafted responses to adaptive challenges and, therefore, failing to create an adaptive culture even as they work hard to do just that. Adaptive work is not simply applying certain techniques to specifically defined challenges. It is about how leaders self-reflect on those default systems of leadership and organizational response that keep working in the background, undermining well-intended responses to adaptive challenges.

The Spirit has now thrust the Eurotribal churches into liminal spaces that demand deep culture change. This is what adaptive change is intended to address. It's more than a new technique applied by the staff of an organization. The power of defaults is to turn the language of "change" (i.e., adaptation, appreciative inquiry) back into another form of existing strategy. Adaptive change requires leaders and people across an organization to risk the transformation of their own default imaginations. They too are implicated in their own adaptation of frameworks and imagination. This is a difficult conversion. One of the best processes for engaging this challenging self-transformation is that of action-learning groups.

Becoming experimenting, resilient, adaptive systems. Only as denominational systems at every level learn to enter together into cooperative experiments shaped around local, distributive networks, they will once more become resilient structures for God's mission in our time. It seems that the Spirit has indeed gone ahead of the church (again) and is out in the midst of the imaginative reframing that is happening in such systems. Denominational systems have much to learn about how to begin forming experiments that invite themselves into the distributive, resilient spaces of changed imagination in which God acts. The Spirit is working in the ordinariness of men and women of faith in local contexts. God's future is gestating among such people who now sense themselves lost in transition. It has been, and always will be, in the local and among ordinary people that the Spirit midwifes new life that forever lies outside the reach of strategic plans, mission statements and existing defaults. Jesus promises to always be with us, ahead and around us on this journey. It is, however, a journey that takes us out of patterned defaults into unfamiliar spaces requiring trust in one another.

The final chapters of this book use Ken Greenberg's reflections on city development to illustrate how this might happen.

Journeying into
the New Space

INTRODUCTION

One way to understand how the proposals outlined in this book might be put into practice is to see them at work in a different setting. This chapter works with Ken Greenberg's engagements with adaptive change as he sought to practice his way into a new imagination for urban centers in North America toward the end of the twentieth century. I will share Greenberg's story of his work in St. Paul, Minnesota, from the mid-1990s forward, and then provide commentary on how this story, in terms of its parallels and applications, applies to the forms of denominational transformation described in this book. I hope that through this exercise you will be given an overall picture of how this change might take place.

Before beginning this story, a final caution is in order against too facile a sense of what is required in cultivating this level of cultural change. Greenberg himself offers a subtext throughout his book that creating and sustaining a new imagination for the revitalization of cities is arduous and difficult work that requires great commitment to a long journey in which one's own self is changed and transformed. This is not easy.

The same needs to be said about the task that now lies before anyone reading this book. Ordinary people who once gave loyalty to their churches and the denominational systems that served them are now deeply disillusioned. They know the churches are not working and have lost faith in the capacities, abilities or willingness of leaders to do anything different from their current practices. They know that the challenges facing the churches have risen to such a level that existing responses won't work, and there's need for a fundamental change of imagination. Existing church systems cannot provide the answers to the challenges facing Christian life in North America. The conviction is increasing that the denominations as they presently function across all levels do not hold the answers to the questions people struggle to address in their contexts. The current mechanisms of denominational life are not competent to address the adaptive challenges the churches face. There can be no doubt that this task of changing the culture and social imaginary of denominational systems will be a demanding journey into new territory. It's going to be very hard work requiring courage and a willingness on the part of leaders to be changed themselves rather than being only the managers of processes they can predict and control.

A TEST CASE: ST. PAUL, MINNESOTA, IN THE EARLY TO MID-NINETIES

Background. By the early 1990s St. Paul's urban center, like so many other cities across North America, was seriously deteriorating. The city was hemorrhaging people, jobs and a confidence that it had a viable, vibrant future. As the downtown experienced decline, the first ring of neighborhoods struggled to maintain a sense of healthy community as commercial life eroded. Other factors contributed to this experience of lost confidence and expectation of a diminished future. St. Paul's twin city, Minneapolis, seemed relatively insulated from these issues as it grew. At the same time, numerous high-profile projects with large amounts of investment had been tried to revitalize the city but hadn't made much difference to its overall trajectory. All in all the citizens and the civic, business and not-for-profit leadership of St. Paul felt very vulnerable.

It doesn't take much imagination to translate this story into that of most denominations at this point in time. The same kinds of experiences, fear and feelings of vulnerability characterize their current situation. As I work with such systems, I invite them to bring together documents describing the initiatives they have launched over the past ten to twenty years to address their own hemorrhaging of people, leaders and resources. As these projects are described, people remember how they were hailed as high-profile answers, developed by smart people at the center, to turn things around. In room after room the response to the question of what happened is the same—little changed. The St. Paul story and the denomination's story are parallel at this point. What did St. Paul do?

Seeking direction, not new plans and projects. In the midst of this crisis the mayor chose a different path from that of yet another big project to turn things around. He invited Ben Thompson, a native son, then a Boston architect, to meet with people to give them assistance in thinking about how to address St. Paul's critical challenges. Thompson didn't develop a master planning document with multiyear goals and benchmarks. He did something counterintuitive. He produced a single watercolor drawing called *The Great River Park* (see fig. 11.1). This was in 1992. It represented a way of focusing attention, a way of inviting people into an imagination that was their own, rooted in the realities and history of the local.

Figure 11.1. The Great River Park

Thompson created a way for people to change the conversation and shift their imagination so that their eyes opened to a different narrative of their neighborhood and, therefore, the possibility of reimagining the urban center and its neighborhoods. As Greenberg makes clear, this remarkable and provocative illustration took enormous liberties by imagining a verdant river valley running through the heart of St. Paul. It turned people's eyes back to the Mississippi, then a degraded and neglected "back" of the city, and set the stage for the next round of creative thinking.[1]

No big development plan was proposed, just a picture that changed a city's imagination. The picture refocused attention on the urban center of St. Paul; it turned people back onto the Mississippi River as the center around which the city had been built and could be renewed again. Thompson understood that through much of the twentieth century it wasn't only suburbanization that hollowed out the inner neighborhoods but something else. The river had become extremely difficult to access. Industrialization and the introduction of large projects based on more modernist perspectives of architecture and city building had practically erased the river from the imagination of the people and the city's own perspectives of itself. The local had been erased for the sake of the general, and the particularity of the life formed by the river was lost behind the screens of development, modernization, one-way streets and eventually a downtown that emptied out after 5 p.m.

A number of insights can be learned from this part of the story. First, while the mayor of St. Paul, along with other concerned citizens, probably had no idea what would emerge from the invitation to Ben Thompson, they understood that in some way there needed to be a different direction; things were getting worse. This is the courage and imagination of leadership. Rather than reacting in fear and trying to come up with one more centered-set project for change, civic leaders left "command and control" for an uncertain journey.

Second, as will be described shortly, a sense that something different had to be tried developed among people at many levels and across differing groups. There was nothing at that point to coalesce this developing instinct, but it was present. In other words, there was a readiness for change even though few could describe what it might look like. Third, Thompson did not act as if he were the heroic leader brought in to save the day and provide the answers. This homegrown architect knew the rhythms of these people and the city from the inside—he was part of the local. What he managed to do was sense, capture and find ways to express the unspoken hunches, intuitions and emerging contours of people in the city. He did this by creating a space within which the gestating imagination could be birthed. His role was not answer person but midwife.

The sketch he produced turned people's eyes to something that was in front of them, but they had lost sight of it in all the wrestling to fix the city out of existing paradigms. This was an immense gift and a key move in starting to change the story of St. Paul. What can't be lost here is that Thompson had seen that the hope for St. Paul's revitalization lay in the local (the river that had been lost to sight and imagination). Further, it is important to note that the mayor caught what Thompson was up to—he sensed that this return to the river was the right way to go. This was not a leaderless revolution (there are no such things) but involved some courageous leaders willing to go outside of their own frameworks and capacities to control. It is about leaders who understood that in times of crisis like St. Paul faced, their role was to create the conditions wherein the people themselves might imagine a new future. Inviting Thompson into the conversation, with his grasp of how to shape the table, was a piece of critical leadership at the right moment. This is leadership that has the inner confidence to know they don't have answers or can't sell new projects; instead they trusted the networks of people in local contexts in order to let an alternative future emerge from among them.

Coalitions and networks to rethink and reimagine. This seeding of the work of culture change expanded conversations which in turn gave permission and nourished the work of others who began to enrich this local turn back to the river. Through the creation of a St. Paul Riverfront Corporation an umbrella was formed under which a broad coalition of groups came together across multiple sectors of the city (neighborhood, commercial, political, business, not-for-profit and foundation groups) to address the challenge of not just turning the face to the local (the river) but actually making the changes that would reinvigorate the local and re-create vibrant communities around the river.

It is important to note that these kinds of local coalitions were already germinating. As stated earlier, there was already something happening under the radar of official projects and city plans waiting to break the surface and coalesce in some form of adaptive innovation. The mayor's leadership and Thompson's willingness to refuse to play the role of heroic leader created the environment for these groups and coalitions at the local level to engage with one another in creative ways. There are no tests to tell if this readiness is present or not. Becoming aware of its presence is part gift, part art and part intuition. Culture change is not predicted or managed; it is felt, tested, entered into in the local and only named in retrospect. The old saying 'it's in the water supply" applies here in terms of leadership. This kind of leadership requires a confidence that something is afoot and enough maturity on the part of leaders to stop trying to manage the future. It is the confidence that if one can cultivate the environment among coalitions of groups, something will be birthed among people at the local level that could not be designed inside a strategic plan.

Across the churches and denominations there is no doubt in this writer's mind that these are the circumstances we are living in. Such coalitions at the local are gestating. The denominations are awaiting leaders who can lay down their own agendas and needs to control in order to cultivate these movements of people on the ground.

Huge challenges require broad coalitions. While coalitions were already present in St. Paul, this was a critical time in which the mayor and the team comprising the Riverfront Corporation needed to leverage the trust they had built (their social capital as leaders in the city) to bring people together from across differing networks and interest groups. The challenge was genuinely adaptive in scope. It had to address how to reconnect the city to the river, and in so doing create actions and projects that would revitalize the downtown. Many projects had been tried before and failed. There was little appetite for these approaches. Thompson's vision of the riverfront was before them, but no one knew how to go about making it reality. Greenberg describes how, when he got involved at this juncture, he recognized,

> The scope of this challenge was extremely broad . . . involv[ing] the full gamut of physical, social, economic, and environmental issues. We would need to show some early results to keep momentum going while not losing focus on the long-term challenges. . . . [We had to] assemble a diverse team of interdisciplinary collaborators.[2]

The critical awareness at this juncture was the adaptive nature of the challenge. It was not addressable within existing methods. It was a challenge that could not be managed by focusing on one element of change (e.g., housing or zoning) or setting up a list of priorities to tackle. Something more was required. Experience elsewhere had shown Greenberg ways of engaging such an adaptive challenge without knowing what the actual points of engagement might be or what the actual outcomes might look like.

Across denominations leaders still tend to want to name the problem or define the area that needs to be addressed. They will, for example, focus on elements such as discipleship or church planting, assuming that if these elements are addressed, most other parts of the church will fix themselves. Once these decisions are made by key leaders in denominational staff, it becomes a matter of putting in the correct strategies, spending the requisite amounts of money (usually provided by foundations) and communicating the ways local churches and midlevel judicatories can participate. Greenberg and the coalitions in St. Paul did not take this approach. They understood that this approach doesn't create culture change and fails to address the adaptive challenges because it has already determined what the adaptive challenges are and how they will be addressed. The local people and their leaders then become the requisite resource for making it happen on the ground.

The Greenberg team's approach was the opposite. They didn't define the solutions but set out to put in place a broad coalition of people and groups at the local level. Putting the coalition together was a primary method of creating the frame for culture change. Further, this team was wise enough to know it had to do several things at once. First, they had to keep their eye on the big picture. This was the empowering of local coalitions to name the actions that would create culture change around the return to the river. Second, they understood it was going to be a difficult challenge in terms of people sustaining the energy and trust over the long term, so they looked for ways to create short-term wins so that early results could confirm the method, give coalitions experience in working together, cement trust and build hope for the hard negotiations ahead. This readiness to be patient, trust the process and empower a broad coalition of people across multiple local groups was a critical next step in developing an environment of culture change.

Discovering the method together. Greenberg writes, "The framework began to take shape as a shared narrative, not just a plan and not just a set of projects, but a belief in the power of a collective vision, one that posed some clear challenges to existing practices."[3] The experience of previous engagements in other cities (e.g., Toronto over the previous two decades) as well as confidence in what happens when self-organization in local communities is given the oxygen to thrive resulted in the St. Paul coalitions being able to design their own method for addressing their adaptive challenges: "Building on the strong tradition of community involvement (a critical condition for a successful effort), a method emerged of working through the issues together in collaborative design sessions."[4] Here, again, leadership focused on establishing the conditions whereby this broad coalition could determine together the method it would use to move forward the emerging common imagination about St. Paul. This process wasn't a flat or leaderless process. Rather, it was resourced by an understanding of leadership focused on nurturing the networks and providing framing for carefully developing environments in which the people themselves determined how to move forward.

The method, itself, was not unimportant, but it was secondary to and dependent on the prior work of building a coalition energized by experimentation around a common, emerging narrative about redeveloping St. Paul around its river. But this was not a vision in any normal sense of that word as it is currently used in denominational systems. Those leading this process did not bring a vision they tried to sell, nor did they first set up multiple study groups to work on defining a vision. Rather, these leaders (such as Thompson) were attuned to the narratives of place (here, St. Paul and its neighborhoods) in order to elicit, call forth and give language to something that was already present, albeit not yet expressed. The leaders knew that this focus was already implicitly and diffusely present across multiple networks and therefore needed to be given space to find its voice. (This was what Thompson intuited and brilliantly framed when he produced his watercolor sketch of the river valley.) Without this approach, the method would have produced little change.

Once this commonly owned vision for the city and its river neighborhood began to coalesce, the emerging, commonly developed method became a key driver of the adaptive work that had to be done. Greenberg and his team played the role of assisting and midwifing the coalitions in discerning the method by modeling it in their own work with them. The model they introduced involved a series of design sessions called "charrettes." This is a term used in many kinds of design processes. It is a method of organizing people into working design groups in such a way that the hierarchical notions of expert and authority are replaced by continuing structured engagements conducive to creativity through having teams of diverse people work on common challenges together as equals. This was not a one-off process but rather learning a way of working together. It involved numbers of gatherings in which these coalitions would develop multiple scenarios for approaching each challenge they faced.

A large charrette group working on a common challenge divides into subgroups of diverse people. Each subgroup works on scenarios for responding to a challenge. The subgroups then come back together to present their scenario proposals in an interactive context of dialogue. Out of these scenario-planning processes the group as a whole begins to discover and name the experiments it will select in order to engage the adaptive challenge before them. What is being developed is not just a method for problem solving but a culture of networked, distributive learning that changes the DNA of the groups and the way the city plans and develops.

In Greenberg's story charrette groups became a key method for local neighborhood networks and civic, commercial and business leaders in turning an emerging vision into practical change. Initially, they were introduced as a method to assist these networks to become aware of the condition of the city and how it got that way. The charrettes gave them the means of doing their own action-learning research. This initial work helped them to name the implicit background narratives (defaults and underlying social imaginaries) that continued to shape decisions in the city. Greenberg writes,

> What we saw was a narrative that began with St. Paul evolving in a unique natural setting on the Mississippi River, which had been formed by the distinctive limestone bluffs and the natural upper and lower "landings" on the river. Next came the arrival of the barge fleets and the hardening of the river banks with industrial dockwalls and the rail lines that spurred indus-

trial growth. And then the familiar post-war noose of highways isolating a downtown area of approximately one square mile, which included some fine buildings now surrounded by parking lots. That brought us to the present: nine-to-five Central Business District, which was losing occupants and value; the institutions; the hospitals; and the small residential population of rich and poor and assorted urbanites.[5]

Once inside these narratives charrette work gave them the tools to deepen people's understandings of both the nature and magnitude of the challenges that lay before them in turning Thompson's sketch into practical reality. It was going to require a major shift in social imaginary. This initial work of the charrettes created the spaces for trust to build across coalitions and a new common narrative to emerge. This work then led into the third level of charrette work, where it was now a method people had confidence and familiarity with as they started the hard work of constructing experiments in developing real, on-the-ground projects for remaking the city and its neighborhoods.

This initial work involved brilliant leadership because it introduced and practiced a method that gave back to local people the opportunity to reconnect with their own originating stories in terms of the sources of city life and neighborhoods. Rather than coming in with some new set of outside proposals, this method attended not just to the work of the people but the archaeology of their own stories and their own work as diggers in the accrued dirt that covered up their stories. As people enter into this process for themselves, they are also being empowered to name their stories, to believe again that their locality and their inherent wisdom are critical elements to making the city live again. The method was all about local empowerment, the shaping of networks of learning communities who discovered together, across differences, that they could make things new. In the midst of this iterative process the "implicit shared vision which had to do with returning to the city's river origins took on its own life. People began to understand the magnitude of the vast river valley and its potential to be improved and reinhabited."[6]

Greenberg's team took this coalescing energy of networks and directed them toward several key areas in order to focus energy and give experiments concreteness. The charrettes continued to be a vital element of this new stage. The working group directing the overall process sought simultaneously to provide broad concepts (a big interpretive picture of what was going on) and specific, very local projects (experiments). The local projects offered the opportunity to develop early wins in renewal as well as test the practices that would make the coalitions work in the future (essential for changing DNA). In this process residents and community members themselves began to provide input on how to engage particular elements of their neighborhoods in this change. The broad concept work became a continuing interpretive narrative giving people the bigger picture.

The team was also aware of the importance of visualizing what was happening: "Extremely valuable in this effort was the preparation of overlays on tracing paper . . . which allowed us to get everything on the same page. . . . Through this opportunistic lens, the remarkable difference that a shared vision could make began to come into focus."[7] In terms of architectural design they used the overlay method by producing drawings of communities that displayed neighborhoods as they currently existed, proposed areas for development and drawings of what these developments might look like when completed. They also produced broader overlay drawings of the city center and its surrounding neighborhoods in terms of past, present and proposed developments.

Optimizing and collaborating. St. Paul started to become a different kind of city. The refocusing and reclaiming of the river valley and its neighborhoods resulted in the return of economic and commercial vitality. It changed the DNA of the city and in so doing, some of its narratives and self-perceptions. This was not the result of top-down leadership, nor was it because a heroic leader stamped his or her vision on people. It resulted from leaders with focused attention on people in their local contexts and the provision of processes that resourced the formation of coalitions and networks to address complex, multiple challenges that no linear, lockstep strategy could engage. Leadership did not embark on projects of structural change, nor did they want to deconstruct institutions. Rather, they formed distributed learning networks capable of reflecting on the overall picture of how culture change occurs, and developing practices for pursuing that culture change by focusing down on specific, concrete projects. In this way a network of communities learned that gaining experience in fixing one challenge could lead to another and another and yet another. Distributive clusters of local coalitions became the engines of adaptive change.

Throughout this journey the importance of leadership creating the safe spaces where differing groups could learn to collaborate cannot be underestimated. What was being learned was that substantive, long-term culture change is not a matter of experts knowing what to do and drawing up the plans. From experiences with Jane Jacobs and coalitions of politicians, neighborhood groups and business leaders in Toronto, Greenberg and his team had learned a new way of working, where imagination, direction and the shape of projects emerge from among the people. The skill of leadership is not about being in charge (those with needs to be top dogs need not apply) but in creating the spaces for such collaborative teams to develop in the local. This is not a diminishment of the skills, experience or wisdom experts and professionals bring (they are critical for culture change) but a reimagination of their roles.

Who Needs Structures?

One of my favorite cities is London. I relax by finding a hotel somewhere in the square mile and spend several days walking about the city. I get lost, find new places, sit in a restaurant listening in on conversations and wander like a stranger in a crowd amid the buzz of the city with its incessant movement and mixing of peoples. London, like New York, Hong Kong, Melbourne and Toronto, is a continually creative city. There is a richness and diversity, a veritable tapestry of life woven from all the colors one could imagine with all kinds of fine materials.

On a recent visit on an autumn afternoon I left my hotel near the Canadian Embassy and wandered the city, walking for almost eight hours with a supper stop in an amazing Turkish restaurant around the corner from Harrods. *What is it*, I thought to myself, *that makes this such a vibrant and creative city?* As I looked around an answer came to my question—structure and institutions. I stood on the left bank of the Thames in the early evening watching crowds move back and forth. To my left stood Big Ben and the Houses of Parliament. I had walked past Westminster Abbey and Churchill's statue only a half hour before. As my eyes moved to the right and down the Thames there was the outline of St. Paul's Cathedral standing in the midst of much newer kinds of buildings over in the financial district. At that moment it became clear to me that these structures, these institutions with all their accumulated traditions and the stories they represented (some of which, as an Englishman raised in Liverpool still unsettle me) were not impediments to the London that had grown up around them. The creativity of the city had not been stunted by its structures and institutions. Something quite different was actually going on—these old, sometimes stuffy, often irrational institutions, structures and traditions had formed the background, the frameworks and solid, predictable, ever-present givenness that made for the creativity.

In this sense London, with its capacity to be continually self-creating, is like a group of actors doing improvisation. They are creating, making something up as they go around, from what's been given to them. The creativity in such work can be wonderful, showing off the giftedness of the actor and how she is able to express herself so freely. At the same time, behind that improvisation lies another layer. She expressed those moments of creativity so brilliantly because she has taken the time to apprentice herself to her craft. This means learning from masters who have lived this craft before her (the institutionalization of knowledge, form and experience). She has done this by joining a theater school (another institution) and obediently disciplining herself to learn specific skills (structures), which she practices as she takes parts in plays—some new, many old (traditions). All of these complex levels form the background and stage on which she now improvises her art.

Several years ago I wandered through the financial district of London early on a Sunday evening to visit a small experiment in church life called Moot. Under the leadership of Ian Mobsby, an Anglican priest, Moot was meeting in the old church of St. Mary Aldermary. If you wander about the financial district you might have a hard time finding the old church building. It is lost in the midst of Tube entrances, ancient narrow streets and posh shops selling Gucci, Montblanc and an assortment of other off-the-shelf forms of identity making. Moot is a creative and experimental church that identifies itself as a form of urban monastic order. The small church building, designed by Sir Christopher Wren, was damp and a bit long in the tooth. Pews and other accouterments of the modern mindset shaped its ethos. There was little doubt that this structure had been colonized a long time ago by narratives of power, control and empire. One could easily have dismissed the place as just one more example of these dying institutional forms of church that were no longer of any value in the new, post-everything time. But this would have been to operate out of yet another narrative of power and control. It would have been to colonize oneself to narratives that missed what was happening here. Three other narratives insinuated themselves into these anti-institutional assumptions.

I saw a plaque on one wall of the church building quite near the elevated pulpit and surrounded by memorials to dead soldiers ("glorious dead for God and country"—a problematic narrative of its own). It told me that this was the church where John Newton preached after his conversion. This is the John Newton who wrote the hymn "Amazing Grace." I suddenly realized that here was the place where this man lived among a neighborhood of people and reshaped a church within Anglicanism after God had done something amazing in his life as the captain of a slave ship. As I entered that story and Newton's time, my imagination was filled with questions and ideas about what God might do again in that neighborhood if a group of Christians reentered Newton's narratives and started to improvise them into this time. These structures and institutions would take on new life!

Along part of the opposite wall toward the corner was a small steeple sitting somewhat awkwardly inside the building. Beside it was another plaque. Many buildings were destroyed in London during World War II, and this steeple, if I am remembering correctly, was from one such building. The plaque told me that this particular steeple was one mentioned in one of T. S. Eliot's better known poems about the ennui of modern life in midcentury London. Eliot's poetry pressed into awareness that the legitimating narratives of late modernity had deeply colonized and profoundly wounded the human soul. There, in this structure designed for worship, I was again reminded about the roots of such worship. In the midst of this ruminating, Moot was gathering for worship, the words of institution were being read and, as the wine and bread shared, a young woman was improvising in modern dance as she expressed the biblical story of the prodigal. What about structures and institutions?

It is not that structures and institutions are somehow bad or wrong and need removing, to be replaced with what the latest guru thinks is right for the time. *Institution* is not a pejorative term, a code word for all that is bad and wrong. Some people throw the word *institution* around as

if it were a great curse to human thriving, like the bubonic plague. It is
neither the structure nor the institution that's the problem, but the ways
in which deeper narratives colonize these forms of life. The call of leadership is not to pour energy into obsessing how to change structures and
remake institutions. Rather, it is to wonder together how to invite and
cultivate a movement of people who are ready to change these narratives.
Only then does it become possible to ask rightly about the kinds of structures and institutions we need.

Notes

1 THE PLACE OF STRUCTURES IN THE MIDST OF MASSIVE CHANGE

[1]According to a 2012 article in *Fast Company*, the average worker stays at his or her job for 4.4 years and will have an average of ten to twelve jobs in a lifetime. See Anya Kamenetz, "The Four-Year Career," *Fast Company*, January 12, 2012, www.fastcompany.com/1802731/four-year-career.

[2]Diana Eck, *A New Religious America* (New York: HarperCollins, 2002), pp. 2-3, 4.

[3]Andrew Davison and Alison Milbank, *For the Parish: A Critique of Fresh Expressions* (London: SCM Press, 2010).

2 STRUCTURES EMBODY OUR DEEPLY HELD STORIES

[1]See Niall Ferguson, *The Great Degeneration: How Institutions Decay and Economies Die* (New York: Penguin, 2013).

[2]Dwight Zscheile, *People of the Way: Renewing Episcopal Identity* (Harrisburg, PA: Morehouse, 2012).

[3]Ibid., p. 17.

[4]Ibid., p. 19.

[5]Ibid., pp. 23-24.

[6]See Ulrich Beck, *Risk Society* (Thousand Oaks, CA: Sage, 1992), and Ulrich Beck, *World Risk Society* (Malden, MA: Polity Press, 2008).

[7]See Alan J. Roxburgh, *Missional Map Making* (San Francisco: Jossey-Bass, 2010).

3 STRUCTURE AND INSTITUTIONS

[1]Niall Ferguson, *Civilization: The West and the Rest* (New York: Penguin, 2011), p. xv.

[2]The American Revolution was different. It adopted and embedded itself in some of the key institutional structures that had emerged from the Enlightenment.

[3]See Charles Taylor, *Modern Social Imaginaries* (Durham, NC: Duke University Press, 2004). Ward builds upon Taylor's work.

[4]An excellent illustration of this reality is portrayed in Dave Egger's recent novel *The Circle* (New York: Vintage, 2013).

[5]Graham Ward, *The Politics of Discipleship* (Grand Rapids: Baker Academic, 2009), p. 164.

[6]David Harvey, *Spaces of Hope* (Berkeley: University of California Press, 2000), pp. 12-13.

[7]Jaroslav Pelikan, *Spirit Versus Structure* (New York: HarperCollins, 1968), p. 5.

[8]This is the language used by the House of Bishops of the United Methodist Church in 2011, when they called their churches to action in a process of church revitalization.

[9]Lesslie Newbigin, *Foolishness to the Greeks* (Grand Rapids: Eerdmans, 1988), p. 1.

[10]I am aware that this is never a simple cause-effect relationship. Once narratives incarnate themselves in structures, then a cycle is established wherein each reinforces the other.

4 REEVALUATING STRUCTURE AND SPIRIT

[1]See the discussion of the increasing numbers of people who find themselves in this place in such recent works as Robert Putnam and David C. Campbell, *American Grace* (New York: Simon & Schuster, 2010).

[2]See, Alan J. Roxburgh, *Missional Map-Making* (San Francisco: Jossey Bass, 2010), pp. 146-47.

[3]Here I presume Ephesians is a Pauline text representing his wrestling with the meaning of the Christian narrative in light of Jesus' incarnation, crucifixion and resurrection.

[4]Bryan Stone, *Evangelism After Christendom: The Theology and Practice of Christian Witness* (Grand Rapids: Brazos, 2007), p. 17.

[5]Ibid.

[6]There is a bias built into these questions, namely, toward the local church in all its aspects. When local church is used in this material, it is not limited to the contemporary understanding of local church as some branch office of a denominational system. Rather, local church can refer to any and all forms of Christian gathering in a local context characterized by such things as worship, prayer, Eucharist, a gathering around Scripture and a commitment to a common mission. Local churches do not need to meet in church buildings or be sponsored by other bodies, nor do they need to be led by either paid or ordained clergy. These obviously represent certain forms of local churches that have been dominant in Christendom. The shifting nature of Christian life in the Western context, however, means that local churches can be characterized by a range of models and practices—from denominational franchises to house churches to new monastic orders to many other types of gathering.

[7]In this material a close relationship will be found between structures and rhythms of Christian life. This connection reflects the conviction that the op-

timal structures for missional life are those that invite people into and reso-cialize them through the rhythms and practices of Christian life.

5 LEGITIMATING NARRATIVES: STRUCTURES AND THE CHURCHES IN THE TWENTIETH CENTURY

[1]See Jane Jacobs, *The Birth and Death of Great American Cities* (New York: Random House, 1961); Anthony Flint, *Wrestling with Moses* (New York: Random House, 2009); and Ken Greenberg, *Walking Home* (Toronto: Random House, 2012).

[2]Culture is a multivalent idea. This book cannot give space to the variety of interpretations and definitions of culture available. Because the focus of this work is the organizational culture of denominational systems, it will use the particular description developed by Edgar Schein in his book *Organizational Culture and Leadership* (San Francisco: Jossey-Bass, 1992). Schein offers this definition: "A pattern of shared basic assumptions that the group learned as it solved its problems of external adaptation and internal inte-gration, that has worked well enough to be considered valid and, therefore, to be taught to new members as the correct way to perceive, think, and feel in relation to those problems" (ibid., p. 12). This definition will be dis-cussed in more detail later.

[3]This point is well made by Graham Ward in his important book *Cultural Trans-formation and Religious Practice* (Cambridge: Cambridge University Press, 2005), esp. sec. 2: "How Do Cultures Change?"

[4]See Jürgen Habermas, *Legitimation Crisis* (Boston: Beacon Press, 1975). Habermas has given considerable thought to the question of legitimacy. His book addresses issues of the legitimacy of economic structures, industrialization, capitalism and the role of a reductive, functional rationality in modern culture. He analyzes how legitimation functions in a social system and asks what happens to these systems when confronted by a crisis of their legitimacy.

[5]See Christopher Lasch, *The Triumph of the Therapeutic* (Chicago: University of Chicago Press, 1987).

[6]Habermas, *Legitimation Crisis*.

[7]In terms of the sociocultural shifts see Hugh McLeod, *The Religious Crisis of the 60s* (Oxford: Oxford University Press, 2007).

[8]Habermas, *Legitimation Crisis*, p. 2.

[9]Ibid., p. 4.

[10]See Ronald A. Heifetz and Marty Linsky's discussion of these issues in terms of adaptive and technical challenges in *Leadership on the Line* (Boston: Harvard Business Review Press, 2002).

[11]See Roxburgh, *Leadership, Liminality and the Missionary Congregation* (Har-risburg, PA: Trinity Press International, 1997).

6 CHANGING LEGITIMACY—CHANGING FRAMEWORKS

[1]Stephen Toulmin, *Cosmopolis* (Chicago: Chicago University Press, 1990), pp. 156ff. and Philip Bobbitt, *The Shield of Achilles: War, Peace and the Course of History* (New York: Anchor Books, 2003). Bobbitt would argue that the two great wars of the twentieth century were, in fact, one long war that did not end until the fall of communism around 1989. His view would be that this long war was fought over the question of which form of the nation-state would prevail over its competing forms. Thus, in the twentieth century three such forms were in competition, either directly or through proxies: fascism, communism and democratic capitalism. Only at the end of the twentieth century did the results of that conflict become clear. Each system claimed to be the optimal form of the nation-state in terms of providing its citizens with the government best suited to meet their needs. But both Bobbitt and Toulmin are in agreement that it was the Westphalian agreement that formed the modern world and initiated the development of the modern state. There are other descriptions of the dynamics of these transformations which provide somewhat differing readings. See, for example, Jürgen Moltmann, "Progress and Abyss: Remembrances of the Future of the Modern World," in *The Future of Hope: Christian Tradition and Postmodernity*, ed. Miroslav Volf and William H. Katerberg (Grand Rapids: Eerdmans, 2004), pp. 3-26.

[2]The following descriptions are obviously not a sufficient summary of all the complex forces that have been reshaping the modern experiment through the twentieth century. There is a huge list of books that have been written over the past half century by a wide variety of thinkers seeking to provide explanatory frameworks for the massive dislocations and transformations in modernity. The description in this section acknowledges that it represents a very small angle of interpretation and provides little more than a rough and schematic attempt at locating some, but by no means all, of the reasons why denominational systems find themselves in a deep crisis of legitimacy.

[3]See Bobbitt, *The Shield of Achilles*, pp. 69-205.

[4]See Karl Polanyi, *The Great Transformation: The Political and Economic Origins of Our Time* (Boston: Bacon Hill Press, 1957).

[5]See Adam B. Seligman, *Modernity's Wager: Authority, the Self and Transcendence* (Princeton, NJ: Princeton University Press, 2000), esp. chaps. 1-2.

[6]Toulmin frames this argument in his book especially in terms of Descartes's work and its influence. This turning from the ordinary and everyday to the thinking self was in many ways a reaction to the horrors of the Thirty Years' War, but it also developed because of this new confidence in method and the sense that the enlightened mind could provide a foundational way toward a better world.

[7]Zygmunt Bauman, *Intimations of Postmodernity* (London: Routledge, 1992), p. 10.

[8]See Alan Seligman, *Modernity's Wager: Authority, the Self, and Transcendence* (Princeton, NJ: Princeton University Press, 2003).

[9]Emmanuel Kant described enlightenment as our emergence from self-incurred immaturity. Immaturity, he saw as the inability to use one's own understanding without the guidance of another. Its cause is lack of resolution and courage to think without the guidance of another. The motto of enlightenment was: *Sapere aude!* Have courage to use your own understanding!

[10]Numerous factors, religious and otherwise, contributed to the development of the modern corporation. The point here is limited, namely, that one of the important elements to emerge from a period of massive social and cultural transformation was a new organizational structure that came to be known as the corporation.

[11]Manuel Castells is a professor of sociology who has taught at the University of Southern California and is a member of the European Institute for Innovation and Technology. His major work is the three-volume study *The Information Age: Economy, Society and Culture* (Oxford: Blackwell, 1996-1998). See also Ulrich Beck, Anthony Giddens and Scott Lasch, *Reflexive Modernization: Politics, Tradition and Aesthetics in the Modern Social Order* (Cambridge: Polity Press, 1994), pp. 1-52, and John Ralston Saul, "The Collapse of Globalism and the Re-birth of Nationalism," in *Harper's*, March 2004, pp. 33-43.

[12]This is one of the points being made by Heifetz and Linsky in their conception of *adaptive change*, where the challenges to be addressed are no longer the kinds that can be addressed by experts and professionals alone but require learning communities of people in the local shaped by experiments. See two key books: Ronald Heifetz and Marty Linsky, *Leadership on the Line* (Boston: Harvard Business Review Press, 2002), and Ronald Heifetz, *Leadership Without Easy Answers* (Cambridge, MA: Harvard University Press, 1994).

[13]This has been one of the key insights retrieved by feminist and other so-called contextual theologians.

[14]This point is made over and over again by writers such as Beck and Giddens.

[15]See Bauman and Habermas for this argument regarding an individualization that disembeds people from their life worlds.

[16]See Beck, Giddens and Lasch, *Reflexive Modernization*, pp. 110-121.

[17]Beck's insights at this point are important to our discussion of denominational systems. While individuation has become the dominant mode of life at this point in time, Beck argues that this does not mean people escape into themselves or even a very narrow world. Some of this is taking place and gets institutionalized in certain forms of need-focused church life. It also means that individuals now become the authors of their own biographies which are cobbled together out of a variety of bits and pieces (ibid., p. 13). But this individualization does

not remain private: "It becomes political in a definite, new sense: the individu-alized individuals, the tinkerers with themselves and their world, are no longer the 'role players' of simple classical industrial society" (ibid., p. 16). In other words, the role-formed world of the corporate denominational system has lost its primary resource base in a certain kind of understanding and practice of the individual. Much of the world of denominational systems was built around such a functional role system with its professionals, experts, laypeople, volunteers, commissions, programs and committees. It is rapidly disappearing.

[18]Castells's view here is not that of a minority position. There is sufficient con-sensus across a broad spectrum of intellectuals to build on the notion of change described by Castells. John Lukacs reflects this perspective in the opening of his book: "For a long time I have been convinced that we in the West are living near the end of an entire age, the age began five hundred years ago" (*At the End of An Age* [Hartford, CT: Yale University Press, 2002], p. 3). Castells. *Information Age*

[19]Beck, Giddens and Lasch, *Reflexive Modernization*, p. 57.

[20]This is, in part, the intent of both Bauman's *Liquid Modernity* and Beck's *De-mocracy Without Enemies* (Cambridge: Polity Press, 1998) in describing late modernity in terms of liquid modernity. It is another way of expressing Marx's oft-quoted and borrowed phrase, "all that is solid melts into air." The point is that the solid forms of social interaction that functioned over a certain period of time suddenly lose their legitimacy. The experience of people is the disso-lution, the liminality, of the context.

[21]Habermas's argument in the early sections of *Legitimation Crisis*, while primarily economic in form, is making the same argument as that expressed by Castells.

7 METAPHORS AND IMAGINATION

[1]See Jeffery Sachs, *The Price of Civilization* (New York: Random House, 2011), p. 13.

[2]See Ronald Heifetz and Marty Linsky, *Leadership on the Line* (Boston: Harvard Business Review Press, 2002), pp. 51-74.

8 THE HUB AND SPOKE

[1]Ludwig Wittgenstein, *Philosophical Investigations* 115 (New York: Routledge, 2001).

[2]The reference to experts and professionals is not to denigrate the importance or skills of people trained in a whole host of professions. This is simply not the point, as Ronald Heifetz and many others continue to assert (see also my earlier book, *Missional Map-Making*). The point being made over and over again in this book is that of Heifetz; namely, that in the midst of massive culture change, the adaptive work is of a different kind than the expertise and skills developed within periods of continuous change. To the point being made here, when de-

nominations adapted to the hub-spoke organizational structure, they also came to rely primarily on the skills and leadership of certain kinds of experts and professionals. That world is less and less amenable to the levels and kinds of change that now need to be addressed. This does not mean professionals and experts are unimportant, but it does mean the kind of reliance that has been put on and given to these people will not help these systems engage their disruptive, adaptive contexts.

[3]Craig Van Gelder, "An Ecclesiastical Geno-Project: Unpacking the DNA of Denominations and Denominationalism" in *The Missional Church and Denominations*, ed. Craig Van Gelder (Grand Rapids: Eerdmans 2008), pp. 12-45.

[4]Ibid., p. 43.

[5]Megan McArdle, "Why Companies Fail." *The Atlantic*, March 2012, p. 32.

[6]See section "The Corporate Organizational Culture" in chapter 6.

[7]McArdle, "Why Companies Fail," pp. 28-32.

[8]Ibid., p. 32.

9 CHANGING THE CULTURE OF THE DENOMINATIONS

[1]See Alan J. Roxburgh, *The Sky Is Falling: Leaders Lost in Transition* (Grand Rapids: Baker, 2009).

[2]The program, Together in Mission, can be seen via the link on the Missional Network website: http://themissionalnetwork.com/?s=Together+in+Mission.

[3]The basis for this discussion is found in Chris Turner's *The Leap* (Toronto: Random House, 2011), pp. 100-112; 314-15. For a much broader discussion of these revolutionary transformations in Europe (especially Germany) see Jeremy Rifkin, *The Third Industrial Revolution: How Lateral Power is Transforming Energy, the Economy, and the World* (New York: Macmillan, 2011).

[4]Adaptive work involved bringing local knowledge and expert skills into partnership. Answering the question of how to design and build a house that produces electricity in this manner required new learning from all involved. It needed a combination of local experience along with expert skills (e.g., the application of computer technology to managing electrical flows in a house). Needed resources had to be identified through experimentation that invited the development of new competencies being developed together. There was much unpredictability in the change process, and everyone involved had to become different in one way or another.

[5]See, for example, Paul Sparks, Tim Soerens and Dwight Friesen, *The New Parish* (Downers Grove, IL: InterVarsity Press, 2014).

[6]See Alan J Roxburgh, *Missional—Joining God in the Neighborhood* (Grand Rapids: Baker, 2011).

[7]See, for example, some of the new groupings on the Internet and accessible

through Facebook, such as the Parish Collective, the Starfish Community and Missional Communities.

[8]See Craig Van Gelder video presentation on the stages of denominational life on the Missional Network vimeo channel (https://vimeo.com/37868275).

[9]See Clemens Sedmak, *Doing Local Theology: A Guide for Artisans of a New Humanity* (Maryknoll, NY: Orbis, 2002).

[10]See James McClendon, *Systematic Theology*, vol. 1, *Ethics* (Nashville: Abingdon, 1986), pp. 20-27.

[11]Sedmak, *Doing Local Theology*.

10 FROM HERE TO THERE

[1]See Ronald Heifetz, *Leadership Without Easy Answers* (Cambridge, MA: Harvard University Press, 1994).

[2]For an extensive discussion of leadership see Alan Roxburgh and Fred Romanuk, *The Missional Leader* (San Francisco: Jossey-Bass, 2006).

[3]Jacobs was not a professional architect or city planner. We might say she was an ordinary woman who took the local, everyday and ordinary seriously, thus developing the intuition that human thriving in cities was built around the interactions of hundreds, if not thousands, of people on the street. Her life and work, along with the many who followed after her, helped to form the distributive age in terms of city life.

[4]See Alan Seligman, *The Problem of Trust* (Princeton, NJ: Princeton University Press, 2000).

[5]Adam B. Seligman, *Modernity's Wager: Authority, the Self and Transcendence* (Princeton, NJ: Princeton University Press, 2000), p. 4.

[6]The problem with interpreting Jesus' words about wine and wine skins is the failure to grasp that new wine really isn't that valuable; it has to age before it is worth drinking.

[7]For an extended discussion of this text see Alan J Roxburgh, *Missional: Joining God in the Neighborhood* (Grand Rapids: Baker, 2011).

[8]See Anthony Flint, *Wrestling with Moses* (New York: Random House, 2009).

[9]This focus on the local has been explained in both theological (the ways in which the Spirit gestates new imagination within the ordinary) and sociocultural shifts based on the recognition that big, centered-set projects in hub-spoke designs (sometimes called the big-bang theory of change) cannot engage the challenges that need to be addressed. Such a focus, however, is not intended to romanticize the local or create yet another false polarity between local and midlevel or national organizations. As will be pointed out later, while the local becomes the place where experiments are created, these experiments require new kinds of partnerships and collaborations across the organizational systems

of denominations. It's not that the structures need to be demolished or restructured, but that all of their interrelationships need to be renegotiated. The challenge, however, is that these renegotiations can't be done at the front door; they can only happen on the way, in the midst of experimenting.

[10]See Darrell L. Guder, ed., *Missional Church* (Grand Rapids: Eerdmans, 1998); and Craig Van Gelder, *The Essence of the Church* (Grand Rapids: Baker, 2000).

[11]Ronald Heifetz and Marty Linsky, *Leadership on the Line* (Boston: Harvard Business Review Press, 2002).

11 JOURNEYING INTO THE NEW SPACE

[1]Ken Greenberg, *Walking Home* (Toronto: Random House, 2012), p. 133.

[2]Ibid., p. 137.

[3]Ibid., p. 138.

[4]Ibid., p. 134.

[5]Ibid., pp. 134-35.

[6]Ibid., p. 135.

[7]Ibid., p. 137.

Index

THE
MISSIONAL
NETWORK

A network of leaders across North America and the UK committed to a practical and biblical/theological engagement with the missional conversation in the church.

MISSIONAL PERSPECTIVE

TMN frames its processes, tools, and resources within a robust biblical and theological missional perspective—God's mission in the world and the church's participation in this mission. An organizational understanding of systems is used in relation to these frames to support transformation across local, regional and national church bodies.

RESOURCES FOR TRANSFORMATION

TMN offers a variety of well-tested tools and resources that can help church organizations and their leaders engage in intentional processes of missional innovation and transformation. These resources support the consulting/coaching processes TMN makes available for systems change.

CONSULTING AND COACHING

TMN provides both consulting and coaching to support the transformation of church systems at all levels. The consulting is designed to build the capacity of church systems to engage in systemic missional transformation. The coaching is designed to walk alongside leaders in strengthening their skills and capacities for leading in the midst of change.

PUBLISHING

TMN has a Writing/Publishing Team made up of a broad, cooperative table of church leaders—pastors, teachers, and practitioners that produces a book series and other printed resources to deepen the missional conversation while informing system transformation from a biblical and theological perspective.

TMN ASSOCIATES AND PARTNERS

TMN consists of a team of associates and partners who are part of and have a deep understanding of the historical development of denominations as faith traditions and polities. In all its work this team takes seriously the traditions and histories of each church system viewing it as helpful gift to the larger church.

INTERNATIONAL

TMN is an international organization that works with church leaders in North America, the UK and Europe to understand the particular ways in which the Gospel interacts with the churches and cultures in these locations, with a view towards the transforming of Western cultures.

---

www.themissionalnetwork.com